VICTORIOUS SPIRITUAL SCRIPTURES

DEE BUTLER

BALBOA.
PRESS
A DIVISION OF HAY HOUSE

Balboa Press books may be ordered through booksellers or by contacting:

Balboa Press
A Division of Hay House
1663 Liberty Drive
Bloomington, IN 47403
www.balboapress.com
1 (877) 407-4847

Because of the dynamic nature of the Internet, any web addresses or links contained in this book may have changed since publication and may no longer be valid. The views expressed in this work are solely those of the author and do not necessarily reflect the views of the publisher, and the publisher hereby disclaims any responsibility for them.

The author of this book does not dispense medical advice or prescribe the use of any technique as a form of treatment for physical, emotional, or medical problems without the advice of a physician, either directly or indirectly. The intent of the author is only to offer information of a general nature to help you in your quest for emotional and spiritual well-being. In the event you use any of the information in this book for yourself, which is your constitutional right, the author and the publisher assume no responsibility for your actions.

Print information available on the last page.

ISBN: 978-1-9822-1655-9 (sc)
ISBN: 978-1-9822-1754-9 (e)

Balboa Press rev. date: 01/15/2019

Contemporary English Version (CEV)
King James Version (KJV)
Todays English Version (TEV)

Scripture quotation: taken from the Holy Bible:Contemporary English Version(CEV), Good News Translation(GNT) and the King James Version (KJV) references, concordance Thomas Nelson bible copyright 2003, The MBCC Book store library The views expressed in this book are not necessarily those of the publisher. All rights reserved solely, by the author.

CONTENTS

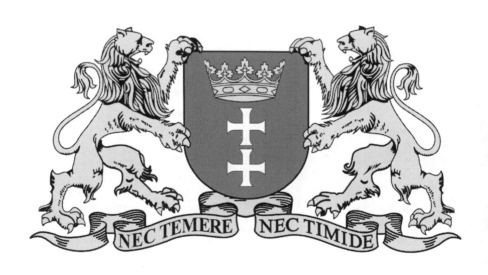

NEC TEMERE NEC TIMIDE

DEDICATION

♪ SPECIAL THANKS

TO THE FATHER, THE SON, AND THE HOLY SPIRIT
To: my Pastor: Rev. J L Turner and my Church Family
THE MISSISSIPPI BOULEVARD CHRISTIAN CHURCH

Special Thanks
To: my loving wife Cheryl:

♪ FAMILY AND FRIENDS

Rev. Tommie Butler, and Missionary Diane Katherine
Mothers: Eula, and Beaulah Emery
Civil Rights Activist Deaconess Earlene Amos
Dr. C. Amos, Henley's Florist, and Attorney S. Holmes

♪ MENTORS

Dr. Alvin O Jackson, Frank A Thomas, Bishop Porter
Apostal Williams, Dr. Frank E. Ray, Dave Ramsey
and the staff of 95.7 Hallelujah FM radio station,
Dr. C. Dollar and Bishop T.D. Jakes

❧ HONORABLES

The late great bishop G.E. Patterson
Mrs. Early Draper Butler
Sgt. Micheal Butler u.s.m.c

❧ THANKS TO

Memphis City and Shelby County Schools for (30) years of service, and The Veterans of America. Proud supporters of Memphis Mental Health, St. Jude, and Le'Bonheurs childrens Hospitals.

Scripture quotation: taken from the Holy Bible:Contemporary English Version(CEV), Good News Translation(GNT) and the King James Version (KJV) references, concordance- Thomas Nelson Bible copyright 2003, The MBCC Book store library.

PREFACE

VICTORIOUS SPIRITUAL SCRIPTURES

There's a war going on, and if you're going to win; You better make sure that you have God's word deep down within. This battle can't be won with bullet's and guns. For the enemy you cannot see with natural eyes, and human faculties. Ephesians=6:12 For we wrestle not against flesh and blood, but against principalities, against power, against the rulers of the darkness of this world, against spiritual wickedness in high places. It's a fact that Satan's on your track and suddenly, without any warning he'll launch his attack. So this is what you have to know, you can't fight this battle on your own you need the power of God's word rooted and grounded in your life. This is what the bible say's: We need the armor of the Holy Ghost, so we can walk right, talk right, live right, and pray right.

Military strategies of war, are to know your weaponry and your enemy advantages, and disadvantages in the natural sense, but in the spiritual war, the war is right between your two ears, the war is fought in your mind; that is why we should have the mind of God. Satan's desire is to control your mind, your will, your thoughts, and your dreams. 2.Corinthians =10:4 For the weapon of our warfare are not carnal, but mighty through God to the pulling down of strong holds; Casting down imaginations, and every high thing that exalted itself against the knowledge of God. Ephesians=6:11 Therefore put on the whole armour of God, that you may be able to stand against the wiles of the devil.

The word is spiritual food, 1Peter=2:1 exhorted us to desire the sincere milk of the word as newborn babies, that we may grow thereby: The word of God is pure, genuine, and unadulterated. To absorb the word of God into our spiritual system will insure protection against all kinds of spiritual disease, sickness, and deformity. The word is food that we need for life, growth, health, and spiritual strength. The word of God is for the people of God. 2 Timothy=3:16 All scriptures are given by inspiration of God: The word of God is life, it's quick and it's powerful, it's truth, it's corrects, it enlightens, it heal, it delivers, and it bring about "results."

The word of God does not return without accomplishing that which it was sent to do. Jeremiah=1:9 God said; behold I have put my words in thy mouth see, I have this day set thee over the nations, and over the Kingdoms.

The word of God is for people who are struggling, and who think God has forgotten about them. The word of God acts as a pain medicine, when you are going through life's situations.

Victorious scriptures helps you to see life through God's eyes. These scriptures are to be used while praying for yourself and others. The scriptures help you to know what to say when you are talking to God, which helps you get results and not just dead words and repetitious prayers. These are scriptures that have helped me over the years of my life, while going through various situations.

The Word of God is, God promises that he gave us to use and to have confidence in him. Where is God when we need him? He's in his Word. Study and know the word.

II Timothy 2:15 Study to show thyself approved unto God, a workman that needed not be ashamed, rightly dividing the word of truth.

The key to life is in the Word of God. What a precious indescribable gift to have. The Word of God which gives us victorious power in love, grace, forgiveness, healing, wealth, faith, authority, hope and in Christ- centered living.

In conclusion, stop being a victim and start being victorious through the word of God. I -Timothy- 6:12 Fight the good fight of faith, lay hold on eternal life.

Webster dictionary states: Victorious = victory, "latin":

Having overcome an enemy: Triumphant, Conquering. Thank you Holy Ghost in the name of Jesus.

B.I.B.L.E. the word Bible signifies-

basic instructions before leaving earth.

VICTORIOUS SPIRITUAL SCRIPTURES

THE LORD'S PRAYER

♫ MATTHEW = 6: 9 KJV

After this manner there for Pray ye:
Our Father which art in Heaven Hallowed be thy name.
Thy Kingdom come, thy will be done on earth, as it is in Heaven. Give us this day our daily bread and forgive us our debts, as we forgive our debtors, and lead us not into temptation, but deliver us from evil; for thine is the kingdom and the Power, and the Glory, Forever Amen.

♫ JESUS FIRST SERMON: LUKE = 4:18 CEV

Jesus read the Scripture from the book of Isaiah the Prophet Chapter 61:1 The Lord's Spirit has come on me because he has chosen me to tell the good news to the poor.
The Lord has sent me to announce freedom for the prisoners, to give sight to the blind to free everyone who suffers, and to say, this is the year the Lord has chosen!

VICTORIOUS SPIRITUAL SCRIPTURES 1

We confess that Jesus is the Christ, The son of the living God, and proclaim Him Lord, and Savior of the world. —MBCC

ROMANS = 8:37 KJV

I am more than a conqueror, through him that love me.

I JOHN = 4:4 KJV

Greater is he that is in me, than he that is in the world.

PHILLIPPIANS = 4:13 KJV

For I can do all things through Christ, which strengtheneth me.

ISAIAH = 54:17 KJV

No weapon formed against me shall prosper and every tongue that shall rise against me in judgement thou shalt condemn.

VICTORIOUS SPIRITUAL SCRIPTURES 2

In Christ's name and by His grace, we accept our mission of witness and service to all people. —MBCC

ROMANS = 8:31 KJV

> If God be for us who can be against us?

ISAIAH = 40:31 KJV

> They that wait upon the Lord shall renew their strength they shall mount up with wings as eagles: They shall run and not be weary and they shall walk and not faint.

PSALM = 121:1 KJV

> I will lift up mine eyes unto the hills from whence cometh my help:
> All my help cometh from the Lord: which made heaven and earth.

NEHEMIAH = 8:10 KJV

> For the joy of the Lord is my strength.

LUKE = 2:10 KJV

> Behold, I bring you good tidings of great joy, which shall be to all people.

VICTORIOUS SPIRITUAL SCRIPTURES 3

We rejoice in God, maker of heaven and earth, and in the covenant of love which binds us to God and one another. —MBCC

✿ PSALM = 37:25 KJV

> I have been young and now I am old; yet have I not seen the righteous forsaken, nor his seed begging bread.

✿ MATTHEW =18:20 KJV

> For where two or three are gathered together in my name, there am I in the midst of them.

✿ JOHN = 14:14 KJV

> If you shall ask anything in my name, that will I do unto you.

✿ 1- THESSALONIANS = 5:16-20 KJV

> Rejoice evermore, pray without ceasing. In everything give thanks for this is the will of God in Christ Jesus concerning you. Quench not the Spirit, despise not prophesyings

VICTORIOUS SPIRITUAL SCRIPTURES 4

Through baptism into Christ, we enter into newness of life and are made one with the whole people of God. —MBCC

☙ MATTHEW = 6: 33 AND LUKE = 12:31 KJV

Seek ye first the kingdom of God and his righteousness; and all these things shall be added unto you.

☙ PROVERB = 3:5 KJV

Trust in the lord with all thine heart and lean not unto thine own understanding:
In all thy ways acknowledge him; and he shall direct thy path

☙ MARK = 11:24 KJV

Therefore I say unto you what things so ever you desire when you pray, believe that you receive them and you shall have them.

☙ PSALM = 103:1 KJV

Bless the Lord, O' my soul: and all that is within me, bless his holy name.

VICTORIOUS SPIRITUAL SCRIPTURES 5

In the communion of the Holy Spirit, we are joined together in discipleship and in obedience to Christ. —MBCC

♫ 2 CHRONICLES = 7:14 KJV

If my people, who called by my name; will humble themselves and pray; seek my face and turn from there wicked ways. Then will I hear from heaven; forgive them of their sins and heal their land.

♫ ISAIAH = 26:3 KJV

Thou will keep him in perfect peace whose mind is stayed on thee,
Trust in the lord JE-HO-VAH forever, for in the lord is everlasting strength

♫ LAMENTATIONS = 3:22 KJV

It is of the Lord's mercies that we are not consumed, because his compassions fail not. They are new every morning:
great is thy faith fullness.

♫ PSALM = 51:10 KJV

Create in me a clean heart, O God; and renew a right spirit within me.
Cast me not away from thy presence; and take not thy holy spirit from me.

♫ 2 CHRONICLES = 20:15 KJV

For the battle is not yours, but it's the Lord.

VICTORIOUS SPIRITUAL SCRIPTURES 6

At the table of the Lord, we celebrate with thanksgiving the saving acts and presence of Christ. —MBCC

ROMANS = 8:28 KJV

> We know that all things work together for good to them who are called according to his purpose.

PSALM = 138:8 KJV

> The Lord will perfect that which concerneth me.

PSALM = 37:23 KJV

> The steps of a good man are ordered by the Lord and he delighteth in his way:

ROMANS = 4:17 KJV

> Calleth those things which be not as though they were. Who against hope believed in hope, so shall thy seed be!

VICTORIOUS SPIRITUAL SCRIPTURES 7

Within the universal church, we receive the gift of ministry
and the light of scripture. —MBCC

🙏 PHILIPPIANS = 3:14 KJV

> I press toward the mark for the prize of the high calling of
> God in Christ Jesus.

🙏 PHILIPPIANS = 4:6 KJV

> Be careful for nothing; but in everything by prayer and
> supplication
> with thanksgiving let your request be made known unto God.

🙏 ECCLESSIASTES = 9:11 KJV

> The race is not given to the swift nor to the strong but to him
> that endureth to the end.

🙏 JOHN = 3:3 AND MATTHEW = 18:3 KJV

> Jesus said: except a man be born again he cannot see the
> kingdom of God!

🙏 MATTHEW = 5:6 KJV

> Blessed are they which do hunger and thirst after righteousness,
> for they shall be filled.

VICTORIOUS SPIRITUAL SCRIPTURES 8

In the bonds of Christian faith, we yield ourselves to God that we may serve the one whose kingdom has no end. Blessing, glory, and honor be to God forever. –MBCC

♫ MATTHEW= 18:19 KJV

> If (2) two of you shall agree on earth as touching; anything that they shall ask;
> It shall be done for them of my Father which is in heaven.

♫ MATTHEW = 18:18 KJV

> What so ever you shall bind on earth shall be bound in heaven,
> What so ever you shall loose on earth shall be loosed in heaven:

♫ EPHESIANS = 1:3 KJV

> Blessed be the God and Father of our Lord Jesus Christ who hath blessed us with all spiritual blessing in heavenly places in Christ Jesus.

♫ PHILIPPIANS = 2:13 KJV

> For it is God which worketh in you both to will and to do of his good pleasure.

Father I stretch my hand to thee, no other help I know.
If thou withdraw thyself from me, O'whither shall I go?
—CHARLES WESLEY

MATTHEW = 11:28 KJV

Come unto me, all ye that labour and are heavy laden, and I will give you rest.
Take my yoke upon you and learn of me; for I am meek and lowly in heart; and ye shall find rest unto your souls. for my yoke is easy and my burden is light.

2 CORINTHIANS = 5:17 KJV

Therefore If any man be in Christ he is a new creature;
Old things are passed away behold all things are become new.

PSALM = 46:1 KJV

God is our refuge and strength a very present help in time of trouble.

ISAIAH = 59:19 KJV

From the rising of the sun even unto the going down of the same.
When the enemy shall come in like a flood, the Spirit of the Lord shall lift up a standard against him.

May the words of my mouth and the meditation of my heart be exceptable in thy sight- O my strength and my redeemer. —Traditional Spirituals

♫ LUKE = 10:18 KJV

> I beheld Satan as lightning fall from heaven.
> Behold, I give unto you power to tread on serpents and scorpions and over all the power of the enemy; and nothing shall by any means hurt you.

♫ PSALM = 91:13 KJV

> Thou shalt tread upon the Lion and the Adder (snake),
> the young Lion and the dragon shalt thou trample under.

♫ JAMES = 4:7 KJV

> Submit yourself therefore to God resist the devil and
> he will flee from you.

♫ PROVERB = 12:21 KJV

> There shall no evil happen to the righteous, but the wicked shall be filled with mischief.

VICTORIOUS SPIRITUAL SCRIPTURES 11

When I think about the goodness of "Jesus, and all that he's done for me, my soul cries out Hallelujah; Thank you Lord, for saving me. — Traditional Spirituals

🔥 2 CORINTHIANS = 5:20 KJV

> Now then we are, Ambassadors for Jesus Christ, Therefore, we are reconciled unto God!

🔥 1 CHRONICLES = 16:22 - PSALM = 105:15 KJV

> Touch not mine Anointed, and do my Prophets no harm.

🔥 PSALM = 34:19 KJV

> Many are the affliction of the righteous, but the Lord delivereth him out of them all.

🔥 ACTS = 17:28 KJV

> For in him we live, and in him we move, and in him we have our being.

🔥 GALATIANS = 3:13 KJV

> Christ hath redeemed us from the curse of the law, being made a curse for us; for it is written, cursed is everyone that hangeth on a tree.

❧ ACTS = 3:25 KJV

You are the children of the prophets, and of the covenant
which God made with our fathers, saying unto Abraham,
And in thy seed shall all the kindreds of the earth be blessed.

VICTORIOUS SPIRITUAL SCRIPTURES 12

Lord, please forgive me of my sins and forgive those who despitefully persecute against me. For vengeance is mine said the Lord. — Traditional Spirituals

♫ LUKE- 10:20 KJV

> Not with standing in this rejoice not
> that the spirits are subject unto you.
> But rather rejoice, because
> your names are written in heaven
> in the lamb book of life.

♫ 2 CORINTHIANS- 5:7 KJV

> For we walk by faith, not by sight.
> We are confident, I say and
> willing rather to be absent from
> the body and to be present with the Lord.

♫ ROMANS- 8:16 KJV

> The Spirit itself beareth witness
> with our spirit, that we are
> the children of God and know
> this that we have an advantage against Satan the devil, and
> it's through the power of the Holy Ghost.

Praise God from whom all blessings flow.
Praise him all creature here below.
Praise him above ye heavenly host.
Praise Father, Son and Holy Ghost. —THOMAS KEN

♫ HEBREWS =12:1 KJV

> Wherefore seeing we also are compassed about
> with so great a cloud of witnesses, Let us lay
> a side every weight and sin which doth so easily
> beset us and let us run with patience the race that is set
> before us.

♫ GENESIS =1:26 KJV

> God said, Let us make man in our image,
> after our likeness; and let them have dominion,
> power and authority over the earth and every living thing that
> moveth upon the earth.

♫ GENESIS =1:27 KJV

> So God created man in his own image,
> in the image of God created he him; male and
> female created he them. And God blessed
> them, and God said unto them.
> Be fruitful and multiply and replenish the earth,
> and subdue it; and have dominion

over the fish of the sea, and over the fowl
of the air, and over every living thing that
moveth upon the earth.

🙏 AMOS 3:3 KJV

Can (2) two walk together except they be agreed?

Amazing grace; how sweet the sound, that saved a wretch like me. I once was lost, but now I am found, was blind, but now I see. — JOHN NEWTON

♪ GENESIS = 2:7 KJV

> The Lord God formed Man of the dust of the ground and breathed into his nostrils the breath of life and man became a living soul.

♪ I CORINTHIANS = 15:44 KJV

> It is sown a natural body. It is raise a spiritual body. There is a natural body and there is a spiritual body.

♪ I CORINTHIANS = 15:45 KJV

> So it is written; the first man Adam was made a living soul. The last Adam, Jesus Christ was made a quickening Spirit...

♪ JOB = 2:1 KJV

> There was a day when the Sons of God came to present themselves before the Lord, and Satan came also among them to present himself before the Lord. and the Lord God said unto Satan, from whence comest thou?

And Satan answered, from going to and fro in the earth, and from walking up and down in it; seeking whom I may devour.

✤ PROVERB = 3:16 KJV

Wisdom offers you length of days is in her right hand; and in her left hand riches and honour.

VICTORIOUS SPIRITUAL SCRIPTURES 15

Holy, Holy, Holy, Lord God Almighty
Early in the morning our song shall rise to thee.
Holy, Holy, Holy, Merciful and Mighty God in (3) three Persons,
Blessed Trinity. —REGINALD HEBER

HEBREWS= 12:2 KJV

> Looking unto Jesus the author and finisher of our faith;
> who for the joy that was set before him endured the cross
> despising the shame, and is set down at the right hand of the
> throne of God.

I CORINTHIANS= 6:19 KJV

> Your body is the temple of the Holy Ghost which ye have of
> and ye are not your own. For you are brought with a price.

I PETER= 5:6 KJV

> Humble yourselves therefore under the mighty hand of God
> that he may exalt you in due time.

PSALM= 46:10 KJV

> Be still and know that I am God. I will be exalted among the
> heathen.

ISAIAH = 40:8 KJV

> The grass withereth, the flower fadeth: but the word of our
> God shall stand forever. The everlasting word of God.

VICTORIOUS SPIRITUAL SCRIPTURES 16

Blessed Assurance Jesus is mine. What a fore taste of Glory Divine Heir of Salvation purchase of God born of His Spirit washed in His Blood.—FANNY J. CROSBY

🎵 2 CORINTHIAN= 10:4 KJV

> For the weapon of our warfare are not carnal, but mighty through God to the pulling down of strongholds casting down imagination and every high thing that exaltheth itself against the knowledge of God.

🎵 EPHESIANS = 6:12 KJV

> For we wrestle not against flesh and blood, but against principalities, against powers, against the rulers of the darkness of this world, against spiritual wickedness in high places.

🎵 HOSEA= 4:6 KJV

> My people are destroyed for a lack of knowledge.

🎵 DEUTERONOMY = 32:30 KJV

> One saint can chase a thousand, and two can put ten thousand demons to flight.

♔ JOHN = 7:37 KJV

Jesus said; if any man thirst, let him come unto me, and drink. He that believeth on me, as the scriptures hath said, out of his belly shall flow rivers of living waters.

♔ JOHN = 4:14 KJV

Who so ever drink of the water that I shall give him shall never thirst;
but the water that I shall give you shall be in you, a well of water springing up into everlasting life.

♔ MATTHEW = 28:20 KJV

Jesus said; I am with you always, even unto the end of the world.

All to Jesus I surrender
All to him I freely give
I will forever love and trust Him
In His presence daily live.—JUDSON W. VANDEVENTER

🙏 I JOHN = 5:14 KJV

> This is the confidence that we have in him. that if we ask
> anything according to His will He heareth us.

🙏 PSALM=37:4 KJV

> Delight thy self also in the Lord and he shall give thee
> the desires of thine heart.

🙏 ROMANS =12:1 KJV

> I beseech you therefore brethren by the mercies of God,
> that you present your bodies a living sacrifice, holy, acceptable
> unto God, which is your reasonable service.

🙏 PHILLIPPIANS =1:6 KJV

> Being confident of this very thing; that he which hath begun a
> good work in you will perform it until the day of Jesus Christ.

🙏 PROVERB = 2:21 KJV

> For the righteous shall dwell in the land, and the perfect shall
> remain in it.

For your goodness and your glory
for the joy inside your story
for the peace you gave to me
for the day you set me free. —JOHN P. KEE

♫ JOHN 10:10 KJV

> Satan, the thief cometh not, but
> for to steal and to kill and to destroy.
> I come that they might have life
> and that they might have it
> more abundantly.

♫ ROMANS= 6:23 KJV

> For the wages of sin is death, but the
> gift of God is eternal life through Jesus Christ.

♫ 2 CORINTHIANS = 5:10 KJV

> For we must all appear before the judgement
> seat of Christ that everyone may receive the things
> done in his body according to that he had done whether
> it be good or bad.

♫ DEUTERONOMY = 28:7 KJV

> The Lord shall cause thine enemies that rise up against thee
> to be smitten before thy face: They shall come out against thee
> one way, and flee before thee seven ways.

Living He loved me
Dying He saved me
Buried He carried my sins far away
Rising He justified, free me forever
One day He's coming back, O' Glorious Day.
—DONNIE MCCLURKIN

JEREMIAH = 33:3 KJV

> Call unto me and I will answer thee,
> and shew thee great and mighty things
> which thou knowest not.

NUMBERS = 6:24 KJV

> The Lord bless thee; and keep thee
> The Lord make his face to shine upon thee
> And to be gracious unto thee.
> The Lord lift up His countenance upon thee,
> and give thee peace

MATTHEW = 22:37 KJV

> Jesus said:
> "Thou shalt love the Lord thy God with all thy heart,
> and with all thy soul and with all thy mind."
> This is the first and great Commandment.

The blood that Jesus shed for me, way back on Calvary.
The blood that gives me strength, from day to day.
It will never lose it's power.—ANDRAE' CROUCH

♫ PSALM = 55:22 KJV

> Cast thy burden upon the Lord, and
> he shall sustain thee; He shall
> never suffer the righteous to be moved.

♫ I PETER = 2:9 KJV

> You are a chosen generation a royal priesthood,
> an holy nation a peculiar people, that ye should
> shew forth the praises of him who hath called you out of
> darkness into his marvelous light.

♫ I CORINTHIANS = 2:9 KJV

> Eyes hath not seen, nor ears heard
> neither have entered into the
> heart of men the things which God
> hath prepared for them that loved him.

♫ MATTHEW = 5:8

> Blessed are the pure in heart: for they shall see God.

♫ HEBREWS= 11:6 KJV

> Without faith it is impossible to please God.

Victory is mine- Victory is mine
Victory today is mine,
I told Satan, get thee behind
Victory today is mine.—DOROTHY NORWOOD

JOHN =14:6 KJV

> Jesus said: "I am the way, the truth and the life:
> no man cometh unto the Father but by me."

JOHN = 3:16 KJV

> For God so loved the world that he gave his
> only begotten Son, that whosoever believeth in Him
> should not perish but have everlasting life.

I CORINTHIANS =15:58 KJV

> Therefore, my beloved brethren
> be ye steadfast unmoveable
> always abounding in the work
> of the Lord forasmuch as ye know that
> your labor is not in vain in the Lord.

JONH = 14:27 KJV

> Peace I leave with you, my peace I give unto you;
> not as the world give, so be not deceived.

♫ JOHN = 4:23 KJV

The hour cometh, and now is, when the true
worshippers shall worship the Father in spirit, and
in truth; for the Father seeketh such to worship him.

♫ LUKE = 1:30 KJV

The angel said; his name is Jesus; He shall be great, and
shall be called the son of the most highest: and the Lord
God shall make him a king, as his ancestor David was, and he
will be the king of the descendants of Jacob forever;
his kingdom will never end!

Pass me not, O gentle savior, hear my humble cry,
While on others thou art calling, do not pass me by.
—FANNY J. CROSBY

❧ GALATIANS = 6:7 KJV

> God is not mocked; for whatsoever a
> man soweth that shall he also reap!

❧ MATTHEW =7:7 KJV

> Jesus said: Ask and it shall be given you.
> Seek and you shall find.
> Knock and it shall be opened unto you.

❧ LUKE = 12:48 KJV

> For unto whomsoever much is given,
> of him shall be much required.

❧ JOSHUA = 25:15 KJV

> Choose you this day whom you will serve:
> but as for me and my house. We will serve the Lord.

❧ PSALM = 50:15 KJV

> Call upon me in the day of trouble:
> I will deliver thee and thou shalt glorify me.

ALPHA and OMEGA
The beginning and the end
God of another chance
Forgiver of my sins.—KEVIN DAVIDSON

♫ PROVERBS = 18:21 KJV

Death and life are in the power of the tongue:
and they that love it shall eat the fruit there of.

♫ ROMANS = 8:6 KJV

For to be spiritually minded is life and peace.
Because the carnal mind
is enmity against God, for it is not subject to the law of God!

♫ I CORINTHIANS = 13:11 KJV

When I was a child, I spoke as a child
I understood as a child,
I thought as a child but when
I became a man, I put away childish things.

♫ GENESIS = 18:14 KJV

Is anything to hard for God!
Is there anything to hard for the Lord!

JOHN = 15:7 KJV

If you abide in me, and my words abide in you,
you shall ask what you will, and it shall be done
unto you.

VICTORIOUS SPIRITUAL SCRIPTURES 24

King of King, Lord of Lord
Prince of Peace, Wonderful Counselor
Keeper of my mind, peace in confusion
Through joy and sorrow, hope for tomorrow.—KEVIN DAVIDSON

♫ ROMANS = 10:9 KJV

> If you confess with your mouth, Jesus is Lord! And
> believe in your heart that God raised him from the
> dead, you shall be saved.

♫ ISAIAH = 55:6 KJV

> Seek the Lord while he may be found, call upon him while
> he is near.
> Let the wicked forsake his way and the unrighteous man his
> thoughts,
> and let him return unto the Lord, and he will have mercy
> upon him ;
> and to our God, for he will abundantly pardon.

♫ ISAIAH = 55:8 KJV

> For my thoughts are not your thoughts, Neither are your ways
> my ways,
> For as the heavens are higher than the earth, so are my ways
> higher than
> your ways, and my thoughts than your thoughts.

✿ DANIEL = 12:1 KJV

At that time shall Michael stand up, the great prince which standeth for
the children of thy people; and there shall be a time of trouble, such as never
was since there was a nation even to that same time: and at that time thy
people shall be delivered, everyone that shall be found written in the book.

✿ DANIEL = 12:2 KJV

Many of them that sleep in the dust of the earth shall awake, some to everlasting life, and some to shame and everlasting contempt.
And they that be wise shall shine as the brightness of the firmament; and they that turn many to righteousness as the stars
forever and ever. The rapture.

My hope is built on nothing less, than Jesus blood and righteousness,
I dare not trust the sweetest frame, but wholly lean on Jesus name.
On Christ the solid rock I stand, all other ground is sinking sand.
—WILLIAM B. BRADBURY

♫ EPHESIANS= 6:11 KJV

> Put on the whole armour of God that you may be able
> to stand against the wiles of the devils.

♫ I PETER =5:8 KJV

> Be sober, be vigilant; because your adversary the devil,
> as a roaring lion, walketh about seeking whom he may devour

♫ ROMANS =12:2 KJV

> Be not conformed to this world, but be ye transformed by the
> renewing of your mind that ye may prove what is that good
> and acceptable, and perfect, will of God.

♫ ROMANS = 8:1 KJV

> There is therefore now no condemnation to them
> which are in Christ Jesus.

♫ JOHN = 15:13 KJV

> Greater love hath no man than this, that a man lay down his
> life for his friends.
> You are my friends, if you do what so ever I command you.

VICTORIOUS SPIRITUAL SCRIPTURES 26

When good men do nothing evil flourishes,
we've learned to fly as birds, we've learned to swim as fish
yet we haven't learned to walk the earth as brothers and sisters.
—DR. MARTIN LUTHER KING, JR.

❧ MARK = 8:36 KJV

> For what shall it profit a man if he shall gain the whole world,
> and lose his own soul.

❧ I TIMOTHY = 6:6 KJV

> Godliness with contentment is great gain, for we brought nothing
> into this world and it is certain we can carry nothing out.

❧ HEBREWS = 4:15 KJV

> For we have not an high priest which cannot be touched with the
> feeling of our infirmities; but was in all points tempted like as we are,
> yet without sin.

❧ HEBREWS = 13:5 KJV

> I will never leave thee, nor forsake you.
> The Lord is my helper and I will not fear what man
> shall do unto me.

Great is thy faithfulness, you keep on loving me.
You keep on blessing me, you keep on keeping me.
—KEVIN DAVIDSON

♫ ROMANS = 8:38 KJV

> For I am persuaded that neither death, nor life, nor angels, nor principalities, nor powers, nor things presents, nor things to come, nor height, nor depth, nor any other creature, shall be able to separate us from the love of God, which is in Christ Jesus our Lord.

♫ 2 CORINTHIANS = 2:11 KJV

> Lest Satan should get an advantage of us;
> for we are not ignorant of his devices.

♫ JOB = 22:28 KJV

> Thou shalt also decree a thing and It shall be established unto you, and the light shall shine upon thy ways.

♫ PSALM = 34:1 KJV

> I will bless the Lord at all times: his praise shall continually be in my mouth.

✿ PSALM = 27:13 KJV

I had fainted, unless I had believed to see the goodness of the Lord in the land of the living.

✿ PSALM = 27:14 KJV

Wait on the Lord: be of good courage, and he shall strengthen thine heart: wait, I say, on the Lord.

Changed my way of walking
Changed my ways of talking
Changed my way of living
Changed my way of giving.
—JOHN P. KEE

♫ PSALM = 68:5 KJV

A mother to the motherless - a father to the fatherless
and a Judge of the widows and orphans.
Is God in his holy habitation.

♫ I CORINTHIANS = 10:13 KJV

There hath no temptation taken you but such as is common
to man; but God is faithful who will not suffer you to be
tempted above that you are able; but will with the temptation
also make a way to escape, that you may be able to bear it.

♫ I JOHN=5:15 KJV

If we know that he hear us, whatsoever we ask,
we know that we have the petitions that we desired of him.

♫ JOB= 13:15 KJV

Though he slay me, yet will I trust in Him.

Some folk would rather have houses and land,
Some folk choose silver and gold,
These thing they treasure and forget about their soul
I've decided to make Jesus my choice. —HARRISON JOHNSON

🙏 I JOHN = 5:13 KJV

> These things have I written unto you that you may believe
> on the name of the son of God; that you may know
> that you have eternal life, and that you may believe
> on the name of the son of God.

🙏 2 CORINTHIANS = 12:9 KJV

> Thus said the Lord; my grace is sufficient for thee,
> for my strength is made perfect in weakness.
> Most gladly therefore will I rather glory in my infirmities,
> that the power of Christ may rest upon me.

🙏 PSALM = 107:8 KJV

> Oh that men would praise the Lord,
> For his goodness and for his wonderful works
> to the children of men.

🙏 PSALM = 107:1 KJV

> Give thanks unto the Lord for he is good,
> for his mercy endureth forever.

O' Beautiful for spacious skies, for amber waves of grain.
For purple mountain majesties, above the fruited plains.
—KATHERINE LEE BATES

♫ PSALM = 107:2 KJV

Let the Redeemed of the Lord say so,
whom he hath redeemed from the hand of the enemy.

♫ ROMANS = 11:33 KJV

Oh the depth of the riches both of the wisdom and knowledge of God!
How unsearchable are his Judgments and unfathomable his ways.
For who has known the mind of the Lord or who has become his counselor?
Or who has given back to God all that he has given unto us,
The earth, the moon, and the stars in the sky.
How can we ever repay him for his salvation and his redeeming sacrifice.
For of him and through him and to him are all things are made!
To whom be glory, and honor forever. Amen

♫ MATTHEW = 4:4 KJV – DEUTERONOMY = 8:3 KJV

JESUS said; It is written, man shall not Live on bread alone,
But on every word that comes from the mouth of God.

✤ PHILLIPPIANS = 3:20 KJV

We are citizens of heaven and are eagerly waiting for our savior to come from there.
Our Lord Jesus Christ has power over everything. For he will change our mortal bodies into immortal glorious bodies, like his own.

✤ TITUS = 2:13 KJV

Looking for that blessed hope, and the glorious appearing of the great God and our Saviour Jesus Christ.

✤ PSALM = 47:1 KJV

O' clap your hands all ye people; shout unto God with the Voice of Triumph. ALLELUIA!

America, America
God shed His grace on thee
crown thy good with brotherhood
from sea to shining sea.—KATHERINE LEE BATES

🙏 ISAIAH= 29:13 KJV

Wherefore the Lord said, forasmuch as this
people draw near me with their mouth, and
with their lips do honor me, but have removed
their heart far from me and their fear toward me
is taught by the precept of men.

🙏 ISAIAH= 30:1 KJV

Woe to the rebellious children, saith the Lord, that take
counsel, but not of me; and that cover with a covering, but not
of my Spirit that they may add sin to sin.

🙏 ISAIAH= 43:2 KJV

I am the Lord thy God I have called thee by thy name, thou
art mine.
When thou passest through the waters, I will be with thee;
and through the rivers,
they shall not overflow thee: when thou walkest through the
fire, thou shalt not be
burned; neither shall the flame kindle upon thee.

If when you give the best of your service,
Telling the world that the savior is come,
Be not dismayed, when men don't believe you,
He'll understand, and say well done!—LUCIE EDDIE CAMPBELL

2 PETER = 3:8 KJV

Be not ignorant of this (1) one thing that (1) one day is with the Lord as a thousand years and a thousand years as (1) one day.

JOHN= 1:1 KJV

In the beginning was the Word and the Word was with God and the Word was God. The same was in the beginning with God. All things were made by him: and without him was not anything made that was made.

I JOHN = 4:20 KJV

If a man say I love God, and hated his brother he is a liar: for he that loveth not his brother whom he have seen, how can he love God whom he have not seen.

I TIMOTHY = 6:17 KJV

Charge them that are rich in this world, that they be not high minded, nor trust in uncertain riches, but in the living God, who giveth us richly all things to enjoy.

Tragedies are common place, many kinds of diseases, people are slipping away. Economy down, people can't get enough pay; but as for me, all I can say is, Thank you Lord for all you've done for me. —WALTER HAWKINS

🙏 HEBREWS = 11:6 KJV

> Without faith it is impossible to please him: for he that cometh to God must believe that he is and that he is a rewarder of them that diligently seek him.

🙏 ROMANS = 5:1 KJV

> Therefore being justified by faith we have peace with God through our Lord Jesus Christ.

🙏 EPHESIANS = 2:8 KJV

> For by grace are you saved through faith and that not of yourselves It is the Gift of God.

🙏 HEBREWS = 10:23 KJV

> Let us hold fast the profession of our faith without wavering; for he is faithful that promised.

🙏 HEBREWS = 10:25 KJV

> Not forsaking the assembling of ourselves together, as the manner of some is but exhorting one another.

I can make a man from clay
A universe with words I say
Breathe and part the sea
and out live eternity.—VIRTUE

HEBREWS= 10:38 KJV

Now, the just shall live by faith but, if any man drawback;
my soul shall have no pleasure in him!

GALATIAN = 3:11 KJV

No man is justified by the law in the sight of God.
It is evident for; the Just shall live by faith.

ROMANS = 1:17 KJV

For therein is the righteousness of God revealed from faith to
faith as it is written: The just shall live by faith.
The Just Shall Live by Faith.

HABAKKUK = 2:4 KJV

Behold, his soul which is lifted up is not upright in him;
but the just shall live by his faith.

HABAKKUK= 2:2 KJV

The Lord answered me, and said write the vision, and make it
plain upon tables that he may run that readeth it.

Great is thy faithfulness, God my father,
there is no shadow of turning with thee.
Thou changest not, thy compassions they fail not,
as thou hast been thou forever wilt be.—THOMAS O. CHISHOLM

☙ JOHN =11:25 KJV

Jesus said: I am the resurrection, and the life: he that
believeth in me, though he were dead, Yet shall he live:
And whosoever liveth and believeth in me shall neverdie.
Believest thou this!

☙ I PETER = 4:18 KJV

If the "righteous" scarcely be saved,
Where shall the ungodly and the sinner appear?
Scarcely= means barely made it.

☙ ROMANS = 1:16 KJV

For I am not ashamed of the gospel of Jesus Christ:
For it is the power of God unto salvation to everyone that
believeth:
To the Jew first, and also to the Gentiles.
For therein is the righteous of God revealed from faith to faith:
As it is written, the just shall live by Faith.

❧ PROVERB = 18:24 KJV

A man that hath friends must shew himself friendly; and there is a friend that sticketh closer than a brother.

❧ HEBREWS = 2:3 KJV

How then shall we escape, if we neglect, this great salvation. The message given to our ancestors by the angels was shown to be true.

God confirmed unto us by bearing witness both with signs, and wonders, and with all kinds of miracles, and gifts of the Holy Spirit.

Homeless, living on the streets
Drug habits, they just can't beat.
Muggers and robbers, no place seem to be safe,
but you've been my protection every step of the way.
Thank you Lord for all you've done for me.—WALTER HAWKINS

♫ 2 TIMOTHY = 2:15 KJV

Study to shew thyself approved
unto God, a workman that needeth not
to be ashamed, rightly dividing the word of truth.
But shun profane and vain words.

♫ MATTHEW = 5:16 KJV

Let your light so shine before men,
that they may see your good works
and glorify your Father which is in heaven.

♫ 2 TIMOTHY = 1:7 KJV

For God hath given us the power of love and
of a sound mind; not the spirit of fear.

♫ HEBREWS = 11:1 KJV

Now faith is the substance of things hoped for
the evidence of things not seen.

HEBREWS = 4:16 KJV

Let us therefore come boldly unto the throne of grace
that we may obtain mercy and find grace to
help in time of need.

If you're walking down the right path and you're willing
to keep walking, eventually you'll make progress.
—PRESIDENT BARACK OBAMA (yes we can)

🙏 JUDE = 1:24 KJV

> Now unto Him that is able to keep you from falling and to
> present you faultless before the presence of His Glory with
> exceeding Joy.

🙏 JUDE = 1:25 KJV

> To the only wise God our Saviour, be glory and majesty,
> dominion and power, both now and forever Amen.

🙏 HEBREWS = 10:35 KJV

> Cast not away therefore your confidence, which hath great
> recompence of reward.

🙏 HEBREW = 10:36 KJV

> For you have need of patience, that after you have done the
> will of God you might receive the promise.

🙏 COLOSSIANS = 1:11 KJV

> Being strengthened with all power according to his glorious
> might,
> So that you may have great endurance and patience.

VICTORIOUS SPIRITUAL SCRIPTURES 38

You may build great cathedrals large or small,
you can build skyscrapers grand and tall,
you may conquer all the failures of the past,
but only what you do for Christ will last.
Remember only what you do for Christ will last.
—MAHALIA JACKSON

꩜ PHILIPPIANS = 4:4 KJV

> My fellow labourers, whose names are in the lambs book of
> life.
> Rejoice in the Lord always, and again I say rejoice.
> Let your moderation be known unto all men, the Lord is at
> hand.

꩜ JAMES = 1:5 KJV

> If any of you lack wisdom let him ask of God, that giveth to all
> men liberally, and it shall be given him. Let him ask in faith,
> nothing wavering.

꩜ JAMES = 1:8 KJV

> A double minded man is unstable in all his ways.

꩜ PSALM = 119:11 KJV

> Thy word have I hid in mine heart that I might not sin against
> thee.

Open thou mine eyes, that I may behold wondrous things out
of thy word.

❧ NUMBERS = 23:19 KJV

God is not a man, that he should lie; neither the son of man
that he should repent;
hath he said, and shall he not do it or hath he spoken, and shall
he not make it good?
What God has blessed the enemy cannot curse.

VICTORIOUS SPIRITUAL SCRIPTURES 39

Beams of heaven, as I go through this wilderness below,
Guide my feet in peaceful ways, Turn my midnights into days.
—CHARLES ALBERT TINDLEY

꙳ MARK = 16:16-18 KJV

> He that believeth and is baptized shall be saved, but
> He that believeth not shall be damned, and these signs
> shall follow them that believe; In my name shall they cast
> out devils; they shall speak with new tongues,
> they shall take up serpents; and if they drink any deadly thing,
> it shall not hurt them. They shall lay hands on the sick, and
> they shall recover.

꙳ JAMES = 1:19 KJV

> Wherefore, my beloved brethren let every man be swift to hear,
> slow to speak, slow to wrath; for the wrath of men worketh not
> the righteousness of God.

꙳ JAMES = 1:22 KJV

> Be ye doers of the word and not hearers only, deceiving your
> own selves.

꙳ REVELATION = 22:1-2 KJV

> The angel showed me a river that was crystal clear, and it's
> waters gave life.

The river came from the throne where God, and the lamb were seated.

Then it flowed down the middle of the city main street.

On each side of the river are trees that grow a different kind of fruit each month of the year. The fruit gives life, and the leaves are used as medicine to heal the nation.

GENESIS = 50:20 KJV

You thought evil against me; but God meant it unto my good. Blessed to be a blessing!

VICTORIOUS SPIRITUAL SCRIPTURES 40

What a friend we have in Jesus, all our sins and griefs to bear.
What a privilege it is to carry, everything to God in prayer.
—JOSEPH M. SCRIVEN

♫ JEREMIAH = 17:10 KJV

> I the Lord search the heart I try the reins, even to give every man according to his ways and according to the fruit of his doings.

♫ JOHN = 6:37-39 KJV

> All that the Father giveth me shall come to me, and him
> that cometh to me I will in no wise cast out.
> For I came down from heaven, not to do mine own will, but the will of him that sent me,
> This is the Father's will which hath sent me, that of all which He hath given me I should lose nothing but should raise it up again at the last day.

♫ PSALM = 119:71 KJV

> It is good for me that I have been afflicted; that I might learn thy statutes.

♫ PSALM = 119:105 KJV

> Thy word is a lamp unto my feet and a light unto my pathway.

What peace we often forfeit, what needless pain we bear.
All because we do not carry, everything to God in prayer.
—JOSEPH M. SCRIVEN

🙏 I JOHN = 4:8 KJV

> God is love, he that loveth not knoweth not God, for God is
> Love!

🙏 I JOHN = 4:6 KJV

> We are of God: he that knoweth God heareth us; he that is
> not of God heareth not us, hereby know we the spirit of truth.

🙏 I JOHN = 4:12 KJV

> No man hath seen God at any time, if we Love one another.
> God dwelleth in us, and his love is perfected in us.

🙏 I JOHN = 4:3 KJV

> Every spirit that confesseth not that Jesus Christ is come in
> the flesh is not of God;
> This is that spirit of antichrist, where of you have heard that it
> should come and even now already is it in the world.

🙏 JOHN = 14:12 KJV

> He that believeth on me, the works that I do shall he do also;

and greater works than these shall he do.

🙏 I JOHN = 3:2 KJV

Beloved, now are we the sons of God, and it doth not yet appear what we shall be; but we know that, when he shall appear, we shall be like him; for we shall see him as he is.

VICTORIOUS SPIRITUAL SCRIPTURES 42

If you think education is expensive, wait until you
see how much ignorance cost.
We didn't come to fear the future, we came to shape it.
—PRESIDENT BARACK OBAMA

🙏 I JOHN = 4:1 KJV

> Beloved, believe not every spirit, but try the spirits whether
> they are of God; because many false Prophets are gone out
> into the world.

🙏 I JOHN = 4:13 KJV

> Hereby know we that dwell in Him and He in us, because
> He hath given us of His spirit.

🙏 I JOHN = 4:15 KJV

> Whosoever shall confess that Jesus Christ is the son of God,
> God dwelleth in him and he in God.

🙏 I JOHN = 4:17 KJV

> Here in is our love made perfect, that we may have boldness in
> the day of judgment, because as He is so are we in this world.
> Perfect love casteth out fear.

Oh when the saints go marching in
Oh when the saints go marching in
I want to be in that number
When the saints go marching in. —STEPHEN KEY

🎵 1 JOHN = 5:4 KJV

> For whatsoever is born of God
> over cometh the world: and
> This is the victory that over cometh
> the world, even our faith.

🎵 1 JOHN = 5:8 KJV

> For there are three (3) that bear record in heaven,
> the Father, the Word (son) and the Holy Ghost:
> and these three are (1) one. And there are three that
> bear witness in the earth, the Spirit, and the water,
> and the blood: and these three agree in one.

🎵 1 JOHN = 5:11 KJV

> This is the record that God hath given to us eternal life, and
> this life is in his Son. He that hath the son hath life; and he
> that hath not the son of God hath "not" life. These things have
> I written unto you that believe on the name of the Son of God;
> that ye may know that you have eternal life.

🙏 PSALM = 116:12 KJV

What shall I render unto the Lord for all his benefits toward me?

🙏 ECCLESIASTES =11:5 KJV

As thou knowest not what is the way of the Spirit, nor how the bones do grow in the womb of her that is with child; even so thou knowest not the works of God who maketh all.

Swing Low, Sweet Cha-riot
coming for to carry me home.
I looked over Jordan, What'd I see
a band of angels, coming after me. —ROBERT NATHANIEL DETT

🙏 GALATIANS = 5:1 KJV

> Stand fast therefore in the liberty
> where with Christ hath made us free
> and be not entangled again with the yoke of bondage

🙏 MARK = 10:29 KJV

> Jesus said: There is no man that hath left house, or
> brethren, or sister, or father or mother or wife or
> children or lands, for my sake, and the gospel,
> But he shall receive an hundred fold.
> Nowin this time, houses and brethren and sister and mother
> and children and lands, with persecutions; and in the world
> to come eternal life.

🙏 MARK = 10:31 KJV

> But many that are first shall be last; and the last first.

🙏 MATTHEW = 5:14 KJV

> You are the light of the world. A city that is set on a hill cannot
> be hid.

♫ JOHN = 14:26 KJV

Jesus said:

The comforter, which is the Holy Ghost, whom the Father will send in my name, he shall teach you all things, and bring all things to your remembrance, what so ever I have said unto you.

Must Jesus bear the cross alone,
And all the world go free,
No, there's a cross for everyone,
And there's a cross for me. —THOMAS SHEPHERD

GALATIANS = 4:5 KJV

To redeem them that were under the law,
that we might receive the adoption of sons.
And because you are sons; God hath sent forth the Spirit
of his Son into your hearts crying, Abba Father.

GALATIANS = 4:7 KJV

Wherefore thou art no more a servant, (slave) but a son;
and if a son then an heir of God through Christ.

GALATIANS = 5:16 KJV

Walk in the Spirit and ye shall not fulfil the lust of the flesh.
If we live in the spirit, let us also walk in the spirit.

MARK= 10:14 KJV - MATTHEW = 19:14 KJV

Jesus said unto them, suffer the little children
to come unto me, and forbid them not: for of such is
kingdom of heaven.

JOHN = 16:12 KJV

Jesus said:

I have much more to tell you, but now it would be to much for you to bear. When, however, the Spirit comes, who reveals the truth about God, he will lead you into all the truth. He will not speak on his own authority, but he will speak of what he hears and will tell you of things to come, he will give me glory, because he will take what I say and tell it to you, all that my Father has is mine; that is why I said that the Spirit will take what I give him, and tell it to you.

Precious Lord take my hand, lead me on, help me stand.
I am tired, I am weak, I am worn, thru the storm, thru the night.
Lead me on to the light, take my hand, precious Lord, lead me home.
—THOMAS A. DORSEY

HEBREWS = 6:4 KJV

> For it is impossible for those who were once enlightened, and have tasted of the heavenly gift, and were made partakers of the Holy Ghost and have tasted the good word of God, and power of the world to come. If they shall fall away, to renew them again unto repentance.

HEBREWS = 6:13 KJV

> For when God made promise to Abraham, because He could swear by no greater, He swear by himself saying, Surely blessing I will bless thee, and multiply thee, and so, after he had patiently endured he obtained, the promise.

HEBREWS = 6:17 KJV

> Where in God willing more abundantly to shew unto the heirs of promise the immutability of his counsel confirmed it by an oath; that by two immutable things, in which it was impossible for God to lie.

❧ 2 CORINTHIANS = 5:6 KJV

Therefore we are always confident, knowing that, whilst we are at home in the body, we are absent from the Lord.

❧ 1 THESSALONIANS = 5:23 KJV

The very God of peace sanctify you wholly; and I pray God your whole spirit and soul and body be preserved blameless unto the coming of our Lord Jesus Christ.

Oh' Lord my God, when I in awesome wonder; consider all the worlds thy hands have made. I see the stars, I hear the rolling thunder. Thy power throughout the universe displayed. Then sings my soul, my savior God to thee. How Great thou Art! How Great thou Art!
—STUART K. HINE

❧ MATTHEW = 10:6 KJV

Go rather to the lost sheep of the house of Israel and as you go preach saying, the kingdom of heaven is at hand. Heal the sick, cleanse the lepers, raise the dead, cast out devils; freely ye have received, freely give. Provide neither gold, nor silver, nor brass in your purses, for the workman is worthy of his meat.

❧ MATTHEW = 10:28 KJV

Fear not them which kill the body, but are not able to kill the soul: but rather fear him which is able to destroy both soul and body in hell.

Are not (2) two sparrows sold for a farthing? and (1) one of them shall not fall on the ground without your father, but the very hairs on your head are all numbered. You are more value than many sparrows!

Lift every voice and sing, till earth and heaven ring.
Let our rejoicing rise, High to the listening skies.
—JAMES WELDON JOHNSON

♫ GALATIANS = 4:22 KJV

For it is written; That Abraham had (2) two sons, the one by a slave-girl, the other by a free woman. But he who was of the slave-girl, was born after the flesh; but he of the free woman was by promise. Which things are in an allegory: For these are the two covenants; the one for the Mount Sinai which gendereth to bondage, which is Hagar. But Jerusalem which is above is free, which is the mother of us all. So then, brethren, we are not children of the slave-girl, but of the free woman for Hagar is Mt. Sinai in Arabia.

♫ GALATIANS = 4:25 KJV

For this Hagar is Mount Sinai in Arabia and answereth to Jerusalem which now is, and is in bondage with her children. But as then he that was born after the flesh persecuted him that was born after the spirit even so it is now!

♫ ZECHARIAH = 4:6 KJV

This is the word of the Lord, not by might, nor by power; but by my Spirit, saith the Lord of hosts.

✿ ZECHARIAH = 4:10 KJV

For who hath despised the day of small things? For they shall rejoice, and shall see, the eyes of the Lord, which run to and fro through the whole earth.

It could've been me, outdoors, no food, no clothes,
all alone without a friend, another number, with a tragic end.
—WALTER HAWKINS

♫ MATTHEW = 19:5 KJV

> For this cause shall a man leave father and mother,
> and shall cleave to his wife: and they (2) twain shall be
> (1) one flesh: Wherefore they are no more
> (2) twain, but (1) one flesh. What therefore God hath joined
> together, let not (no) man put asunder.

♫ EPHESIANS = 5:25 KJV

> Husbands love your wives, even as Christ also loved the
> church.

♫ EPHESIANS = 5:23 KJV

> For the husband is the head of the wife even as Christ is the
> head of the church; wives, submit yourselves unto your own
> husbands, as unto the Lord.

♫ I PETER = 3:7 KJV

> Husband dwell with them according to knowledge, giving
> honour unto the wife, as unto the weaker vessel, and as being
> heirs together

of the Grace of Life; that your prayers be not hindered! That your prayers be not hindered!

✿ NUMBERS = 12:1 KJV

Moses, second wife was an Ethiopian woman from east Africa.

VICTORIOUS SPIRITUAL SCRIPTURES 50

Joy to the world the Lord is come. Let earth receive her King
Let every heart prepare Him room and heaven and nature sing.
—ISAAC WATTS

EPHESIANS = 3:20 KJV

Now unto him that is able to do exceeding abundantly above
all that we ask or think, according to the power that worketh
in us.
Unto him be glory in the church by Christ Jesus throughout
all ages, world with end. Amen.

PSALM = 8:4 KJV

What is man: that thou art mindful of him?
And the son of man, that thou visitest him?
For thou hast made him a little lower than the angels and hast
crowned him with glory and honour.
Thou madest him to have dominion over the works of thy
hands; thou hast put all things under his feet.
All sheep and oxen, yea and the beast of the field;
The fowl of the air and the fish of the sea and whatsoever
passeth through the path of the seas. O Lord our Lord how
excellent is thy name in all the earth.

PSALM = 27:4 KJV

One thing have I desired of the Lord, that will I seek after;
that I may dwell in the house of the Lord all the days of my life,
to behold the beauty of the Lord, and to enquire in his temple.

I sing because, I'm happy. I sing because I'm free.
For His eye is on the sparrow and I know He watches me.
—CIVILLA D. MARTIN

🎵 EPHESIANS = 1:17-21 KJV

> That the God of our Lord Jesus Christ. The Father of glory, may give unto you the spirit of wisdom and revelation in the knowledge of him: The eyes of your understanding being enlightened; that you may know what is the hope of his calling and what the riches of the glory of his inheritance in the Saints, and what is the exceeding greatness of his power toward us. Who believe, according to the working of his mighty power, which he wrought in Christ, when he raised him from the dead, and set him at his own right hand in the heavenly places. Far above all principality, and power, and might, and dominion, and every name that is named, not only in this world, but also in that which is to come: And hath put all things under his feet, and give him to be the head over all things to the church. Amen. Selah

🎵 REVELATION = 3:20 KJV

> Behold, I stand at the door, and knock; if any man hear my voice, and Open the door, I will come in to him, and will sup with him, and he with me.

I THESSALONIANS = 4:13 KJV

God wants us to understand how it will be for those followers who have already died. Then you won't grieve over them and be like people who don't have any hope. We believe that Jesus died and was raised to life. We also believe that when God brings Jesus back again, he will bring with him all who had faith in Jesus before they died. Our Lord Jesus told us that when he comes, we won't go up to meet him ahead of his Saints who have already died.

PROSPEROUS SPIRITUAL SCRIPTURES 52

The keys to a long happy healthy life is, to be yourself, do your best and don't let money, people or problems control your happiness. —FARRIS HILL

 III JOHN = 1:2 KJV

> Beloved I wish above all things that thou mayest prosper and be in health even as thy soul prospereth.

PHILIPPIANS = 4:19 KJV

> My God shall supply all my needs according to his riches in glory by Christ Jesus.

ISAIAH = 48:17 KJV

> Thus saith the Lord, thy Redeemer, The Holy One of Israel; I am the Lord thy God which teacheth thee to profit (to get rich) which leadeth thee by the way that thou shouldest go.

I KINGS = 2:3 GNT

> Obey all his laws and commands, as written in the law of Moses, so that wherever you go you may prosper in everything you do.

If you want something, that you never had, you've got to do something that you've never done. —FARRIS HILL

 I - CHRONICLES = 22:13 KJV

Then shall thou prosper, If thou takest heed to fulfil the statutes and judgement which the Lord charged (Moses) with, concerning Israel.

 PROVERBS = 13:22 KJV

A good man leaveth an inheritance to his children's children, and the wealth of the wicked is laid up for the just.
The righteous shall be made fat.

JAMES =1:17 KJV

Every good gift and every perfect gift is from above and cometh down from the father.

EZEKIEL = 28:4 KJV

With thy wisdom and with thy understanding thou hast gotten thee riches, and hast gotten gold and silver into thy Treasures.

 GALATIANS =3:14 KJV

That the blessing of Abraham might come on the Gentiles through Jesus Christ; that we might receive the promise of the Spirit through faith, for Christ hath redeemed us from the curse of the law.

Happiness don't have to, come at the end of the road, you can have it alone the way. —FARRIS HILL

 JOSHUA = 1:8 KJV

> This book of the law shall not depart out of thy mouth; but thou shalt meditate there in day and night that thou mayest observe to do according to all that is written there in: For then thou shalt make thy way prosperous and then thou shalt have good success.

 PSALM = 112:2 KJV

> The generation of the upright shall be blessed, wealth and riches shall be in his house, and his righteousness endureth forever.

 PROVERB = 10:22 KJV

> The blessing of the Lord, It maketh rich, and addeth no sorrow with it.

 DEUTERONOMY = 28:13 KJV

> The Lord shall make thee the head, and not the tail, and thou shalt be above only, and thou shalt not be beneath.

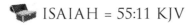 ISAIAH = 55:11 KJV

So shall my word be that goeth forth out of my mouth: it shall not return unto me void, but it shall accomplish that which I please, and it shall prosper in the thing whereto I sent it.

ESTHER = 4:14 KJV

For thou has called thee to come into the kingdom for such a time as this.

PROSPEROUS SPIRITUAL SCRIPTURES 55

A journey of a thousand miles must begin with a single step.
—FARRIS HILL

 PROVERBS= 8:18 KJV

> Riches and honour are with me: yes durable riches and
> righteousness: my fruit is better than gold, yes than fine gold:
> and my revenue than choice silver.

PSALM = 30:6 KJV

> In my prosperity I said, I shall never be moved.
> Lord, by thy favor thou hast made my mountain to stand
> strong:

DEUTERONOMY = 8:18 KJV

> Thou shalt remember the Lord thy God. For it is he that giveth
> thee power to get wealth.

PROVERBS = 8:21 KJV

> I cause those that love me to inherit substance and I will fill
> their treasures.

ECCLESIASTES = 11:1 GNT

> Invest your money in foreign trade, and one of these days you
> will make a profit. Put your investment in several places.

PROSPEROUS SPIRITUAL SCRIPTURES 56

Today is going to be better than yesterday and tomorrow is going to be better than today. —FARRIS HILL

 PROVERBS = 3:9 KJV

> Honor the Lord with thy substance and with the first fruits of all thine increase; so shall thy barns be filled with plenty and thy presses shall burst out with new wines.

 LUKE = 6:38 KJV

> Give and it shall be given unto you: Good measure, press down and shaken together and running over shall men give into your bosom. For with the same measure that you mete withal it shall be measured to you again.

 DEUTERONOMY = 16:17 KJV

> Every man shall give as he is able according to the blessing of the Lord thy God which he hath given thee.

 PSALM = 47:4 KJV

> He shall choose our inheritance for us.

HEBREWS = 11:8 KJV

By faith Abraham, when he was called to go out into a place which he should, not knowing whither to go, received an inheritance for obeying God.

Somewhere in the future you look much better than you look right now! —FARRIS HILL

 II CORINTHIANS = 9:6 KJV

> He which soweth sparingly shall reap also, sparingly: and he which soweth bountifully shall reap also bountifully. Everyman according as he purposeth in his heart: so let him give, not grudgingly or of necessity for God loveth a cheerful giver...

I CHRONICLES = 29:17 KJV

> I know also my God that thou triest the heart and hast pleasure in uprightness. As for me, in the uprightness of mine heart I have willingly offered all these things, and now have I seen with joy thy people, which are present here to offer willingly unto thee O Lord.

2 CORINTHIANS = 4:7 KJV

> We have this treasure in earthen vessels, that the excellency of the power may be of God, and not of us.

2 PETER = 1:3 KJV

> According as his divine power hath given unto us all things that pertain unto life and godliness, through the knowledge of him that hath called us to glory and virtue:

The key to dying empty is to live a full life, vision, purpose, potential leadership and responsibility. —FARRIS HILL

 DEUTERONOMY = 15:10 KJV

> Thou shalt surely give him, and thine heart shall not be grieved, when thou givest unto him: because that for this thing the Lord thy God shall bless thee in all thy works, and in all that thou puttest thine hand unto.

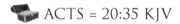 ACTS = 20:35 KJV

> I have shewed you all things how that so labouring ye ought to support the weak, and to remember the words of the Lord Jesus, how He said it is more blessed to give than to receive.

ECCLESIASTES = 10:19 KJV

> A feast is made for laughter, and wine maketh merry: but money answereth all things.

PSALM= 84:12 KJV

> O' Lord of host, Blessed is the man that trusteth in thee.

PROVERBS =22:4 GNT

> Have reverence for the Lord, be humble, and you will get riches, honor, and a long life.

The greatest injustice you can do to yourself and others is not to live up to your full potential. —FARRIS HILL

EPHESIANS =1:11 KJV

> In whom also we have obtained an inheritance being predestinated according to the purpose of him who worketh all things after the counsel of his own will.

EPHESIANS = 3:20 KJV

> Now unto him that is able to do all that we ask or think, according to the power that worketh in us.

GALATIANS =6:7-8-9 KJV

> Be not deceived; God is not mocked: for whatsoever a man soweth, that shall he also reap. For he that soweth to his flesh shall of the flesh reap corruption; but he that soweth to the spirit shall of the spirit reap life everlasting. And let us not be weary in well doing for in due season we shall reap if we faint not.

MATTHEW =14:19 KJV - MARK = 6:41 KJV

> Jesus, took the two fish, and the five loaves of bread, looked up to heaven, blessed it, and gave thanks to God. He broke the loaves and gave them to his disciples to distribute to the people. The number of men who were fed was five thousand. Little becomes much when you place it in the master hand.

PROSPEROUS SPIRITUAL SCRIPTURES 60

So don't deprive yourself of what you can be due to a lack of spiritual dedication and preparation. —FARRIS HILL

 JOSHUA = 6:19 KJV

> All the silver and gold, and vessels of bass and iron are consecrated unto the Lord: They shall come into the treasury of the Lord.

 PSALM= 35:27 KJV

> Let the Lord be magnified which hath pleasure in the prosperity of his servant.

 JOB= 36:11 KJV

> If they obey and serve God; they shall spend their days in pleasure.

 PROVERBS = 18:22 CEV

> Whoso findeth a wife findeth a good thing and obtaineth favor of the Lord. A man's greatest treasure is his wife.
> She is a gift from the Lord!

 PROVERBS = 11:24 CEV

> Sometimes you can become rich by being generous generosity will be rewarded.

Realize your full potential; maximize life to its fullest. —FARRIS HILL

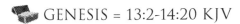 GENESIS = 13:2-14:20 KJV

> Abraham was very rich, in cattle, silver and gold.
> He gave King Melchzedak. The king of Salem; who is the
> Priest of the Most High God.
> Tithes of all, and no one could defeat him in battle.
> All his children was prosperous, forever.

 2 CORINTHIANS = 9:8 KJV

> God is able to make all grace abound toward you; that you
> always having all sufficiency in all things.
> May abound to every good work.

 2 CORINTHIANS = 9:10 KJV

> Now he that ministereth seed to the sower both minister bread
> for your food, and multiply your seed sown and increase the
> fruits of your righteousness:
> Sow your seed; (don't eat your seed!)

 2 CORINTHIANS = 9:11 KJV

> Being enriched in everything to all bountifulness which
> causeth through us thanksgiving to God.

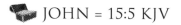 JOHN = 15:5 KJV

I am the vine, you are the branches: He that abideth in me, and
I in him, the same bringeth forth much fruit:
for without me you can do nothing.

 MATTHEW = 5:13 KJV

You are the salt of the earth: Salt is valuable.

Your self-worth is determine by your willingness to invest in who you are, you only get out of yourself what you put in. —FARRIS HILL

ISAIAH = 45:2 KJV

> I will go before thee and make the crooked places straight, I will break into pieces the Iron Gate and I will give you treasures of darkness and hidden riches of secret places, that thou mayest know that I the Lord which call thee by thy name am the God of Israel.

MATTHEW = 6:20 KJV

> Lay up for yourselves Treasures in Heaven where neither moth nor rust doth corrupt and where thieves do not break through nor steal. For where your treasure is there will your heart be also.

PROVERBS = 15:6 KJV

> In the house of the righteous is much treasure; but in the revenues of the wicked is trouble.

I KINGS =1:37 KJV

> As the Lord hath been with my Lord the king, even so be he with Solomon, the richest man ever lived, and make his throne greater than the throne of my Lord king David.

Don't let someone else negative opinion of you become your reality.
It's what you think about yourself that matters most.
—FARRIS HILL

DEUTERONOMY = 28:1 KJV

If thou shalt hearken diligently unto the voice of the lord
thy God,
He will set thee on high above all nation of the earth;
and all the blessing of the Lord shall come on thee, and
overtake thee.

I CHRONICLES = 16:29 KJV

Give unto the Lord the glory due unto his name;
Bring an offering and come before him;
worshiping the Lord in the beauty of holiness.

EXODUS = 23:19 KJV

The(First) of the first fruits of thy land thou shalt bring into
the house of the Lord thy God.

ROMANS = 8:32 KJV

He that spared not his own son, but delivered him up for us all.
How shall he not with him also freely give us all things?

 PROVERB = 6:6 KJV

SEED TIME AND HARVEST/SOWING AND REAPING

Be wise and study the Ant. They have no leader, chief, or ruler, but they store up their food during the summer, and take vacation in the winter. Consider her ways!

Stop making excuses and start making improvements your I -will- is more important than your I.Q. —FARRIS HILL

 DEUTERONOMY = 29:29 KJV

> The secret thing belong unto the Lord our God, but those things which are revealed belongs unto us and to our children forever that we may do all the words of this Law.

DEUTERONOMY = 28:12 KJV

> The Lord shall open unto thee his good treasure;
> the heaven to give the rain unto thy land in his season;
> and to bless all the work of thine hand;
> and thou shalt lend unto many nation and thou shalt not borrow.

PROVERBS = 22:7 KJV

> The rich ruleth over the poor and the borrower is (slave), servant to the lender.

ROMANS = 13:8 KJV

> Owe no man anything, but to love one another;
> For he that loveth one another hath fulfilled the Law.

Education is your, passport into your future,
Tomorrow belongs to those who prepare for it today.
—FARRIS HILL

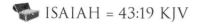 ISAIAH = 43:19 KJV

> Behold I will do a new thing! Now it shall spring forth;
> shall you not know it: I will even make a way in the wilderness
> and rivers in the desert.

PSALM =118:23 KJV

> This is the Lord's doing: and it's marvelous in our sight.
> Lord I beseech thee send now prosperity.

PROVERBS = 14:23 KJV

> Hard work is worthwhile, but empty talk will make you poor.
> Wisdom can make you rich; but foolishness leads to more
> foolishness.

PSALM = 94:14 KJV

> For the Lord will not cast off his people, neither will he forsake
> his inheritance.

LUKE = 1:37 KJV

> For with God nothing shall be impossible!

Your will to win should be exceeding your willingness to prepare. Winners are those who have failed, but they refused to quit.
—FARRIS HILL

PSALM = 84:11 KJV

For the Lord God is a sun and shield, the Lord will give grace and glory, no good thing will He withhold from them that walk uprightly.

LUKE = 16:10 KJV

Anyone who can be trusted in little matters can also be trusted in important matters. But anyone who is dishonest in little matters will be dishonest in important matters. If you cannot be trusted with this wicked wealth, who will trust you with true riches and if you cannot be trusted with what belongs to someone else, who will give you something that will be your own.

DEUTERONOMY = 6:11 KJV

The Lord God shall give thee great and goodly cities, which thou buildedst not. And houses full of all good things, which thou filledst not, and wells digged, which thou diggedst not, vineyards and olive trees, which thou plantedst not; when thou shalt have eaten and be full.

 PROVERBS = 14:34 KJV

Righteousness exalteth a nation, but sin is a reproach to any people.

 JOHN = 13:29 KJV

Jesus, accountant was, Judas Iscariot. He was in charge of the money bag. They thought, Jesus had said unto him, buy those things that we have need of against the feast; or that he should give something to the poor.

There are (3) three kinds of people:

1. Those who let things happen
2. Those who watch things happen
3. Those who make things happen

—FARRIS HILL

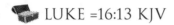 LUKE =16:13 KJV

> Thus saith the Lord Jesus Christ! No servant can serve (2) two masters: for either he will hate the one, and love the other: or else he will hold to the one, and despise the other, you cannot serve God, and mammon.

LUKE = 16:9 KJV

> Thus saith the Lord Jesus Christ: Make to yourselves friends of the mammon of unrighteousness; that when you fail, they may receive you into everlasting habitations.

DANIEL = 11:32 KJV

> Such as do wickedly, against the covenant shall he corrupt by flatteries: but the people that do know their God shall be strong, and do exploits.

MARK = 12:41 KJV

Jesus sat over against the treasury, and beheld how the people cast money into the treasury; and many that were rich cast in much.

PROVERBS = 19:8 GNT

Do yourself a favor and learn all you can; then remember what you have learned, and you will prosper.

PROSPEROUS SPIRITUAL SCRIPTURE 68

It's not where you live that determine who you are
It's what living in you that determines where you are.
—FARRIS HILL

🎒 PHILIPPIANS = 4:11 KJV

Not that I speak in respect of want for I have learned in whatsoever state I am, therewith to be content. I know both how to be abased, and I know how to abound everywhere and in all things. I am instructed both to be full and to be hungry, both to abound and to suffer need. Be ye content.

🎒 JEREMIAH = 29:11 KJV

For I know the thoughts that I think toward you, saith the Lord, thoughts of peace, and not of evil to give you great success. Then shall you call upon me and you shall go and pray unto me and I will hearken unto you, and you shall seek me, and find me, when you shall search for me with all your heart.

🎒 2 PETER = 3:9 KJV

The Lord is not slack concerning His promises, as some men count slackness...

🎒 PSALM = 1:1 KJV

Blessed is the man that walketh not in the counsel of the ungodly, nor standeth in the way of sinners, nor sitteth in the seat of the scornful. But his delight is in the law of the Lord;

and in his law doth he meditate day and night. And he shall be like a tree planted by the rivers of water, that bringeth forth his fruit in his season; his leaf also shall not wither; and whatsoever he doeth shall prosper.

It's not enough that others believe in you what matters most is that you believe in yourself. —FARRIS HILL

 II CHRONICLES = 1:7 KJV

> GOD BLESSED SOLOMON;
> In that night did God appeared unto Solomon, and said unto him. Ask what I shall give thee, and Solomon saith unto God, give me now wisdom and knowledge, that I may go before thy people, and be a great judge for thy people that is so great: And God said to Solomon, because this was in thine heart and thou hast not asked riches, wealth or honour, nor the life of thine enemies, neither yet hast asked long life; but hast asked wisdom and knowledge for thy self, that thou mayest judge my people over whom I have made thee King. Wisdom and knowledge is granted unto thee! and I will give thee riches, and wealth and honour, such as none of the Kings have had that have been before thee. Neither shall there any after thee have the like...

I CHRONICLES = 29:12 KJV

> Both riches and honour comes of thee, and thou reignest over all; and in thine hand is power and might; and in thine hand it is to make great, and to give strength unto all.

I CHRONICLES = 29:11 KJV

Thine, O Lord, is the greatness, and the power, and the glory, and the victory, and the majesty; for all that is in the heaven and in the earth is thine; thine is the kingdom, O Lord, and thou art exalted as head above all.

PROVERBS =18:16 KJV

A man's gift maketh room for him, and bringeth him before great men.

Great minds talk about ideas, average minds talk about events, and small minds simply talk about other people... —FARRIS HILL

PROVERBS = 13:11 KJV

Money wrongly gotten will disappear bit by bit; money earned little by little will grow and grow-not getting what you want can make you feel sick but a wish that comes true is a life giving tree.

HEBREWS = 13:5 KJV

Let your conversation be without covetousness; and be content with such things as ye have: For he hath said; I will never leave thee, or forsake thee.

JOSHUA = 24:13 KJV

I have given you houses, and land for which you did not build, and cities which you built not, and you dwell in them; of the vineyards and olive trees which you planted not do you eat.

DEUTERONOMY = 15:6 KJV

The Lord will bless you as he has promised. You will lend money to many nations, but you will not have to borrow from any. You will have control over many nations, but no nation will have control over you.

PROVERBS = 24:14 KJV

So shall the knowledge of wisdom be unto thy soul; when thou has found it. Then there shall be a reward, and thy exceeded expectation shall not be cut off.

While others are looking at what they are going through winners always look at what they are coming to...... —FARRIS HILL

 2 CORINTHIANS = 8:9 KJV

> For ye know the grace of our Lord Jesus Christ, that, though he was rich: Yet for our sake he became poor, that you through his poverty might be rich.

2 CORINTHIANS = 8:2 KJV

> How that in a great trial of affliction the abundance of their joy and their deep poverty abounded unto the riches of their liberality.

2 CORINTHIANS = 8:14 KJV

> But by an equality that now at this time your abundance may be a supply for their want, that their abundance also may be a supply for your want, that there may be equality.

2 CORINTHIANS = 8:15 KJV

> As it is written: he that had gathered much had nothing over, and he that had gathered little had no lack.

 JOHN = 15:16 KJV

You have not chosen me, but I have chosen you, and ordained you, that you should go and bring forth fruit, and that your fruit should remain; that what so ever you shall ask of the Father in my name, he may give it to you.

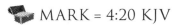 MARK = 4:20 KJV

These are they which are sown on good ground; such as hear the word; and receive it, and bring forth fruit, some thirtyfold some sixty, and some an hundred fold.

All dreams can come true if you have the courage to pursuit them; keep everything easy, effective and enjoyable. —FARRIS HILL

2 CORINTHIANS = 9:12 KJV

For the administration of this service not only supplieth the want of the saints, but is abundant also by many thanksgiving unto God.

2 CORINTHIANS = 9:13 KJV

Whiles by the experiment of this ministration they glorify God for your professed subjection unto the gospel of Christ and for your liberal distribution unto them and unto all men.

2 CORINTHIANS = 9:14 KJV

And by their prayers for the exceeding grace of God in you thanks be unto God for his unspeakable gift.

PROVERBS = 6:31 GNT

When Satan the thief steals from you, he must repay back (7) seven times; he must lose everything that which was stolen and whosoever is under his authority.

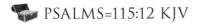

The Lord hath been mindful of us; he will bless us;
He will bless the house of Israel;
He will bless the house of Aaron. He will bless them that fear the Lord both small and great. The Lord shall increase you more and more. You and your children
You are blessed of the Lord which made heaven and earth.

Walk with me, I'll be your guide, Let me lead you to the other side.
—OLETA ADAMS

MATTHEW= 25:14-30 KJV

The kingdom of heaven is also like what happen when a man went away and put his (3) three servants in charge of all he owned. The man knew what each servants could do. So he handed five thousand coins to the (1st) servant, two thousand coins to the (2nd) second servant, and one thousand to the (3rd) third. Then he left the country.

As soon as the man had gone, the servant with the five thousand coins used them to earn five thousand more. The servant who had two thousand coins did the same with his money and earned two thousand more. But the servant with one thousand coins dug a hole and hid his master's money in the ground. Sometime later the master of those servants returned. He called them in and asked what they had done with his money. The servant who had been given five thousand coins brought them in with the five thousand that he had earned. He said, "Sir, you gave me five thousand coins, and I have earned five thousand more." "Wonderful!" his master replied. "You are a good and faithful servant. I left you in charge of only a little but now I will put you in charge of much more. Come and share in my happiness. Next the servant who had been given two thousand coins came in and said, "Sir, you gave me two thousand coins, and I have earned two thousand more." "Wonderful!" his master replied. "You are a good and faithful servant. I left you in charge of only a little, but now I will put you in charge of much more. Come and share in my happiness."

The servant who had been given one thousand coins then came in and said, "Sir, I know that you are hard to get along with. You harvest what you don't plant and gather crops where you have not scattered seed. I was frightened and went out and hid your money in the ground. Here is every single coin!" The master of the servant told him, "You are lazy and good for nothing! You know that I harvest what I don't plant and gather crops where I have not scattered seed. You could have a least put my money in the bank so that I could have earned interest on it." Then the master said," Now your money will be taken away and given to the servant with ten thousand coins! Everyone who has something will be given more, and they will have more than enough. But everything will be taken from those who don't have anything. You are a worthless servant and you will be thrown out into the dark where people will cry and grit their teeth in pain."

What a fellowship, what a joy divine, leaning on the everlasting arm.
What a blessedness, what a peace is mine, leaning on the everlasting arm.
—ELISHA A. HOFFMAN

MALACHI = 3:8 KJV

Will a man rob God? Yet you have robbed me. But you say,
wherein have we robbed thee: In tithes and offering. You
are cursed with a curse: For you have robbed me, even this
whole nation. Bring ye all the tithes into the storehouse, that
there may be meat in mine house and prove me now herewith
saith the Lord of hosts, If I will not open you the windows of
heaven, and pour you out a blessing, that there shall not be
room enough to receive it, and I will rebuke the devourer for
your sakes, and he shall not destroy the fruits of your ground;
Neither shall your vine cast her fruit before the time in the
field saith the Lord of hosts. And all nations shall call you
blessed; for ye shall be a delightsome land; saith the Lord of
host.

DEUTERONOMY = 15:1 KJV

At the end of every seventh year you are to cancel the debts
of those who owe you money. This is how it is to be done,
everyone who has lent money to a fellow Israelite is to cancel
the debt. He must not try to collect the money; the Lord
himself has declared the debt canceled.

I'll cherish the old rugged cross, till my trophies at last I lay down; I will cling to the old rugged cross, and exchange it someday for a crown. —GEORGE BENNARD

 PSALMS = 1:1 CEV

> God blesses those people who refuse evil advice and won't follow sinners or join in sneering at God.
> Instead the law of the Lord makes them happy, and they think about it day and night! They are like trees growing beside a stream, Trees that produce fruit in season and always have leaves. Those people succeed in everything they do.
>
> That isn't true of those who are evil because they are like straw blown by the wind, sinners won't have an excuse on the day of judgment, and they won't have a place with the people of God. The Lord protects everyone who follows him, but the wicked follow a road that leads to ruin, they shall surely perish.

NUMBERS = 11:25 KJV

> The Lord God came down in the cloud and spoke to Moses, He took some of the spirit he had given to Moses, and gave it to the seventy elders. When the spirit came on them, they began to prophesy like prophets, and suddenly the Lord sent a wind that brought quails into the camp, and six hundred thousand men were feed.

Rewards from Jesus for overcomers and those victorious over sin.
Rewards are for those who win the race - The Prize of Eternal Life.

GREAT and GLORIOUS REWARDS:
VARIOUS KINDS of REWARDS:
Great Heavenly rewards
Heavenly rewards
Heavenly Inheritance
Earthly rewards
Earthly Inheritance
1a. The Crown of Life
1b. The Crown of Glory
1c. The Crown of Righteousness
1d. The Crown of Rejoicing
1e. The Incorruptible Crown

MY TRIBUTE: To God be the glory ANDRAE CROUCH
How can I say thanks, for the things you have done for me?
Things so undeserved, yet you gave to prove your love for me.
The voices of a million angels could not express my gratitude.
All that I am, and ever hope to be, I owe it all to thee.

I've taken inventory counted up the cost keeping my eyes on Jesus so I won't get lost. —OLETA ADAMS

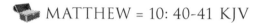 MATTHEW = 10: 40-41 KJV

> He that receiveth you, receiveth me, and he that receiveth me receiveth him that sent me. He that receiveth a prophet in the name of a prophet shall receive a prophet's reward: and he that receiveth a righteous man in the name of a righteous man shall receive a righteous man's reward.

MATTHEW = 10:42 KJV

> Whosoever shall give to drink unto one of these little ones a cup of cold water only in the name of a disciple, verily I say unto you, he shall in no wise lose his reward.

MATTHEW = 5:11 KJV

> Blessed are you when men shall revile you, and persecute you, and shall say all manner of evil against you falsely for my sake. Rejoice, and be exceeding glad: for great is your reward in heaven: for so presecuted they the prophets which were before you.

1 CHRONICLES = 4:10 KJV

> Jabez called on the God of Israel, saying, Oh that thou wouldest bless me indeed, and enlarge my territory, and that thy hand might be with me, and that thou wouldest keep me

from evil, that it may not grieve me! And God granted him that which he requested.

ECCLESIASTES = 5:19 KJV

Every man also to whom God hath given riches, and wealth, and hath given him power to eat thereof, and to take his portion, and to rejoice in his labour; this is the gift of God.

When we all get to heaven, what a day of rejoicing that will be!
When we all see Jesus, we'll sing and shout, and shout the victory!
—ELIZA E. HEWITT

 GENESIS = 15:1 KJV

> After these things the word of the Lord came unto Abram
> in a vision saying: Fear not Abram, I am thy shield and thy
> exceeding great reward...

LUKE = 6:35 KJV

> Respect God's authority: Love your enemies and be good to
> them. Lend without expecting to be paid back, then you will
> get a great reward, and you will be the true children of God
> in heaven. He is good even to people who are unthankful and
> cruel. Have pity on others, just as your Father has pity on you.

PROVERBS = 25:21 KJV

> If your enemies are hungry give them something to eat and
> if they are thirsty give them something to drink. This will be
> the same as pilling hot burning coals on their heads and the
> Lord will reward you.

 REVELATION=21:7 KJV

He that over cometh shall inherit all things; and I will be his God, and he shall be my son.

2 JOHN = 1:8 GNT

Be on your guard, then, so that you will not lose what we have worked for, but will receive your reward in full.

If you want to make the world a better place, Take a look at yourself, and make that, CHANGE! —MICHAEL JACKSON

 MATTHEW = 5:5 KJV

Blessed are the meek: for they shall inherit the earth.

ISAIAH= 40:10 KJV

Behold, the Lord God will come with strong hand, and his arm shall rule for him: behold, his reward is with him and his work before him.

PSALM =19:9-11 CEV

Worshiping the Lord is sacred; He will always be worshiped. All of his decisions are correct and fair. They are worth more than the finest gold and are sweeter than honey from a honeycomb. By your teaching, Lord I am warned; by obeying them, I am Greatly Rewarded.

MATTHEW = 6:1 CEV

When you do good deeds, don't try to show off. If you do, you won't get a reward from your Father in heaven.

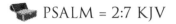 PSALM = 2:7 KJV

I will declare the decree: the Lord hath said unto me. Thou art my son; this day have I begotten thee. Ask of me, and I shall give thee the heathen for thine inheritance, and the uttermost parts of the earth for thy possession.

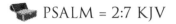 2 CHRONICLES = 32:27 KJV

King Hezekiah became very wealthy, and everyone held him in honour. He had store rooms built for his gold, silver, precious stones, spices, shields, and other valuable objects. He succeeded in everything he did.

Guide our footsteps from sin and shame;
In Christ we're living dying in Christ we gain. —OLETA ADAMS

 COLOSSIANS = 3:24 KJV

> Knowing that of the Lord you shall receive the reward of the inheritance: for you serve the Lord Jesus Christ.

I TIMOTHY = 5:18 KJV

> For the scripture saith: Thou shalt not muzzle the ox that treadeth out the corn, and: the laborer is worthy of his reward.

JEREMIAH= 31:16 KJV

> Thus saith the Lord: Refrain thy voice from weeping, and thine eyes from tears: For thy work shall be rewarded, saith the Lord; and they shall come again from the land of the enemy.

REVELATION =2:9 KJV

> I know thy works, and tribulation, and poverty, (but thou art rich) saith the Lord.

MATTHEW = 16:27 KJV

For Jesus, the son of man shall come in the glory of his Father with his angels; and then he shall reward every man according to his works.

O' how precious is the name of Jesus when you're lonely, heart filled with despair, remember God cares for you, when you're in doubt, can't find your way out, He will see you through. —MYRNA SUMMERS

 MARK= 9:41 KJV

Anyone who gives you a cup of water in my name, just because you belong to me, will surely be rewarded.

I SAMUEL = 2:7-8 KJV

The Lord maketh poor, and maketh rich: he bringeth low, and lifteth up. He raiseth up the poor out of the dust and lifteth up the beggar from the dunghill, to set them among princes, and to make them inherit the throne of glory: for the pillars of the earth are the Lord's and he hath set the world upon them

I SAMUEL 2:9-10 KJV

He will keep the feet of his saints, and the wicked shall be silent in darkness; for by strength shall no man prevail. The adversaries of the Lord shall be broken to pieces; out of heaven shall he thunder upon them; the Lord shall judge the ends of the earth; and he shall give strength unto his king, and exalt the horn of his Anointed.

ACTS = 20:32 KJV

Now, brethren, I commend you to God, and to the word of his grace, which is able to build you up, and to give you an inheritance among all them which are sanctified.

ZECHARIAH = 14:14 KJV

The men of Judah will fight to defend Jerusalem, they will take as loot the wealth of all the nations' gold, silver, and clothing in great abundance.

If you ever need a friend that sticks closer than a brother,
Who'll never ever forsake you, I recommend Jesus, because He's that
kind of friend. —TRAMAINE HAWKINS

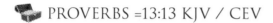 PROVERBS =13:13 KJV / CEV

> Whoso despiseth the word shall be destroyed: but he that
> feareth the commandment shall be rewarded. If you reject
> God's teaching you will pay the price: If you obey his
> commands you will be rewarded...

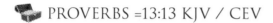 JOHN = 14:2 KJV

> In my father's house are many mansions, if it were not so, I
> would have told you: I go to prepare a place for you, that where
> I am, there you may be also.

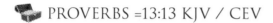 REVELATION=22:12 KJV

> Behold, I come quickly; and my reward is with me, to give
> every man according as his work shall be. I am Alpha and
> Omega, the beginning and the end, the first and the last.

 COLOSSIANS = 1:12 KJV

Giving thanks unto the father which hath made us meet to be partakers of the Inheritance of the saints in light.

I CORINTHIANS = 3:8 KJV

Now he that planteth, and he that watereth are one; and every man shall receive his own reward according to his own.

PROSPEROUS SPIRITUAL SCRIPTURES 83

Galatians= 5:22 KJV Fruits of the Spirit

LOVE
GRACE
LONGSUFFERING
JOY
GENTLENESS
TRUTH
GOODNESS
MERCY
FAITH
RIGHTEOUSNESS
PEACE
TEMPERANCE
HOPE
MEEKNESS

All believers have the fruit of the spirit available to them.
You don't have to ask God for Love, joy, or peace ...
You already have it in you, however you may need to ask for greater yield of your fruit on a day to day basis, The size of the fruit is different among believers.
Some people spend time cultivating their fruit so that it's flourishing, while others tend to neglect their fruit and it becomes unproductive.

The Holy Spirit always given through the laying on of Apostles hands - Acts = 8:14-19 KJV

The Holy Spirit decide who would get which gift in the book of 1Corinthians chapter 12...

SPIRITUAL GIFTS

DISCERNING OF SPIRITS WISDOM

HEALING POWERS

MIGHTY MIRACLES

GREAT FAITH

PROPHECY

KNOWLEDGE

TONGUES

INTERPRETATION OF TONGUES

And through the dark, walking on the sea I saw my Saviour, reaching out to me. —OLETA ADAMS

SPIRITUAL GIFTS

 I CORINTHIANS = 12:1-6 CEV

> Now concerning spiritual gifts, brethren, I would not have you ignorant I want you to remember that before you became followers of the Lord, you were lead in all the wrong ways by idols that can't even talk. Now I want you to know that if you are lead by God's spirits you will say that Jesus is Lord, and you will never curse Jesus. There are different kinds of spiritual gifts, but they all come from the same spirit. There are different ways to serve the same Lord, and we can each do different things. Yet the same God works in all of us and helps us in everything we do. For God is a spirit, and they that worship him, must worship him in spirit and in truth.

I CORINTHIANS = 13:1-13 KJV

> Though I speak with the tongues of men, and of angels, and have not love, I am nothing. And though I have the gift of prophecy, and understand all mysteries, and all knowledge; and though I have all faith, so that I could remove mountains, and have not love, I am nothing. And now there are faith, hope, and love. But of these (3) three, the greatest is love, for God is love.

Love should be your guide. Be eager to have the gifts that come from the Holy Spirit, especially the gift of prophecy. For he that speaketh in an unknown tongue speaketh not unto men, but unto God; for no man understandeth him; howbeit in the spirit he speaketh mysteries. But when you prophesy, you will be understood, and others will be helped. They will be encouraged and made to feel better. By speaking in tongues that others don't know, you help only yourself. But by prophesying you help everyone in the church. I would that you all spoke with tongues, but rather that you prophesied; For greater is he that prophesieth than he that speaketh with tongues, except he interpret, that the church may receive edification. My friends what good would it do if I came, and spoke unknown languages to you and didn't explain what I meant? How would I help you, unless I told you what God had shown me or gave you some knowledge or prophecy or teaching? Since you are eager to have the gifts of the spirit, you must try above everything else to make greater use of those which help to build up the church. The person who speaks in strange tongues, then, must pray for the gift to explain what he says. For if I pray in this way, my spirit prays indeed.

It was you that save me. It was you that raised me.
It was you that kept me. It was you that never left me.
—KEVIN DAVIDSON

SPIRITUAL GIFTS

 I CORINTHIANS = 12:7-11 CEV

> The spirit has given each of us a special way of serving others.
> Some of us can speak with wisdom; while others can speak
> with knowledge but these gifts comes from the same spirit.
>
> To others the spirit has given great faith or the power to heal
> the sick or the power to work mighty miracles.
>
> Some of us are prophets and some of us recognize when
> God's spirit is present. Others can speak different kinds of
> languages, and still others can tell what these languages mean.
> But it is the spirit who does all this and decides which gifts to
> give to each of us.

ACTS = 2:1 CEV

> On the day of Pentecost, suddenly there was a noise from
> heaven like the sound of a mighty rushing wind. It filled the
> house where they were meeting, and the Holy Spirit took
> control of everyone, and they began speaking with other
> tongues, as the Spirit gave them utterance.

ROMANS =8:2 CEV

The Holy Spirit will give you life that comes from Jesus Christ, and will set you free from sin and death. People who are ruled by their desires think only of themselves. Everyone who is ruled by the Holy Spirit thinks about spiritual things. If our minds are ruled by our desires, we will die, But if our minds are ruled by the Spirit, we will have life, and peace. If we follow our desires, we cannot please God. You are no longer ruled by your desires, but by God's Spirit, who lives in you.

I CORINTHIANS = 11:3 CEV

Now I want you to know that Jesus Christ is the head over all men, and a man is the head over a women. But God is the head over Jesus Christ.

I CORINTHIANS =11:7 CEV

Men were created to be like God, and to bring honor to God. Women were created for men, and to bring honor to men.

He turn water into wine, Gave sight to the blind.
Made the lame to walk, and the dumb to talk.
—KEVIN DAVIDSON

SUPERNATURAL CHARISMATA:

 I CORINTHIANS = 2:7-12 CEV

> We speak of God's hidden and mysterious wisdom that God decided to use for our glory long before the world began. The rulers of this world didn't know anything about this wisdom. If they had known about it they would not have nailed the glorious Lord to a cross, God's spirit has shown you everything. His spirit finds out everything, even what is deep in the mind of God. You are the only one who knows what is in your own mind, and God's spirit is the only one who knows what is in God's mind. But God has given us his spirit. That's why we don't think the same way that the people of this world think. That's also why we can recognize the blessings that God has given us.

 PROVERB =18:4 KJV

> The words of a man's mouth are as deep waters, and the well spring of wisdom as a flowing brook.

 PROVERB =20:5 CEV

Counsel in the heart of man is like deep water; but a man of understanding will draw it out.
Someone's thoughts may be as deep as the ocean, but if you are smart you will discover them.

Love lifted me I was sinking deep in sin, far from the peaceful shore
Stained with in, sinking to rise no more, but the master of the sea,
Heard my despairing cry, from the waters lifted me.
—HOWARD SMITH

SUPERNATURAL CHARISMATA:

 I CORINTHIANS = 2:13 CEV

> Every word we speak was taught to us by God's spirit, not by human wisdom. And this same spirit helps us teach spiritual things to spiritual people. That's why only someone who has God's spirit can understand spiritual blessings. Anyone who does not have God's spirit thinks these blessings are foolish. People who are guided by the spirit can make all kinds of judgments, but they cannot be judge by others. The scriptures ask: (Has anyone ever known the thought of the Lord or given him advice: But we understand what Christ is thinking.

ISAIAH = 59:21 GNT

> God said, if you keep my commandments; I will make a covenant with you. I will give you all power, and authority. Your children, and descendants will be blessed as long as they keep my word, and my statues.

JEREMIAH = 3:15 KJV

> I will give you pastors according to mine heart, which shall feed you with knowledge, and understanding.

DANIEL = 12:4 KJV

O' Daniel, shut up the words, and seal the book, even to the time of the end: Many shall run to and fro, and knowledge shall be increased.

Jesus you're my Lord, I will obey your word till your Kingdom come, not my will thine will be done...
—DONNIE MCCLURKIN

Crowns of Rewards in Heaven
The Believer's Reward in Heaven
The Crown of Life

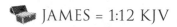 JAMES = 1:12 KJV

> Blessed is the man that endureth temptation: For when he is tried, he shall receive the Crown of Life, which the Lord hath promised to them that love him.

REVELATION = 2:10 KJV

> Fear none of those thing which thou shalt suffer: behold the devil shall cast some of you into prison that you may be tried; and you shall have tribulation ten days: Be thou faithful unto death and I will give thee a Crown of Life.

> The Crown of Life = This is the martyr's Crown, for those who were faithful unto death, those who patiently endured testing, temptations and trials.

DANIEL = 12:13 KJV

> The angel said to Daniel, be faithful to the end. Then you will die, but you will rise to receive your reward at the end of time.

Glory, Glory to the Lamb; You will take us into the land
We will conquer in your name and proclaim that "Jesus Reigns."
—DONNIE MCCLURKIN

Crowns of Reward in Heaven
The Believers Reward in Heaven
The Crown of Glory

 I PETER = 5:2 CEV

> Care for the flock, God has entrusted to you. Watch over it
> willingly, not grudgingly- not for what you will get out of it
> but because you are eager to serve God. Don't Lord it over
> the people, assigned to your care, but lead them by your own
> godly example. And when Christ the Chief Shepherd appears,
> you will receive the crown of glory that does not lose it's glory.

> The Crown of Glory
> The Elder's Crown- This crown is for those leaders, pastors,
> elders, teachers who were Godly examples to the flock of
> believers that were entrusted and assigned to their care.

EPHESIANS = 4:11 KJV

> God gave some to be apostles, and some prophets, and some
> evangelists, and some pastors, and teachers;
> For the work of the ministry, for the edifying of the body of
> Christ.

ISAIAH = 66:22 KJV

> The Lord God said; for as the new heavens and the new earth,
> which I will make, shall remain before me, so shall your seed
> and your name remain.

True is the Lord promises. He's my strength and shield. He help train my hand for war, on life's battlefield. —DONNIE MCCLURKIN

Crowns of Reward in Heaven
The Believers Reward in Heaven
The Crown of Righteousness

 2 TIMOTHY = 4:6 KJV

For I am now ready to be offered, and the time of my department is at hand. I have fought a good fight. I have finished my course, I have kept the faith: Henceforth there is laid up for me a crown of righteousness, which the Lord. The righteous judge, shall give me at that day: and not to me only. But unto all them also that love his appearing.

The Crown of Righteousness: This crown is for those believers who were ready and waiting for the return of Jesus- all those who have loved his appearing.

REVELATION = 3:21 KJV

To him that over cometh will I grant to sit with me in my throne, even as I also overcame, and am set down with my Father in his throne.

REVELATION = 5:12 KJV

Worthy is the lamb that was slain to receive power, and riches, and wisdom and strength, and honour, and glory, and blessing.

He's the Lilly of the Valley, Bright and Morning Star
My enemy's gonna fall, His power conquers all.
—DONNIE MCCLURKIN

Crown of Reward in Heaven
The Believers Reward in Heaven.
The Crown of Rejoicing

 I THESSALONIANS = 2:18 KJV

> Wherefore we would have come unto you, even I Paul, once
> and again; but satan hindered us. For what is our hope, or joy
> or The Crown of Rejoicing? Are not even ye in the presence
> of our Lord Jesus Christ at his coming.

> The Crown of Rejoicing- This is the soul winner's crown- For
> believer's who were obeying Jesus Christ Great Commission.

 PROVERBS = 12:4 KJV

> A virtuous woman is a crown to her husband...

Jesus you're my king, you free me to sing.
I'll praise you all my days, you're perfect in all your ways.
—DONNIE MCCLURKIN

Crown of Rewards in Heaven
The believers reward in Heaven
The Incorruptible Crown

 I CORINTHIANS = 9:24 KJV

> Know ye not that they which run in a race run all, but one receiveth the prize, so run, that you may obtain. And every man/woman that striveth for the mastery is temperate in all things. Now they do it to obtain a corruptible crown; but we obtain an incorruptible crown.

> The Incorruptible Crown
> This is the victors crown for those who disciplined their bodies, and brought their bodies unto subjection- and had self-control...

 I PETER = 1:4 KJV

> To an inheritance incorruptible, and undefiled, and that fadeth not away, reserved in heaven for you.

THE BEATITUDES

Blessed are the poor in spirit for theirs is the kingdom of Heaven.

Blessed are they that mourn for they shall be comforted.

Blessed are the meek: for they shall inherit the earth.

Blessed are they which do hunger and thirst after righteousness: for they shall be filled.

Blessed are the merciful; for they shall obtain mercy.

Blessed are the pure in heart: For they shall see God.

Blessed are the peacemakers for they shall be called the Children of God.

Blessed are they which are persecuted for righteousness sake: for theirs is the Kingdom of Heaven.

Blessed are ye, when men shall revile you, and persecute you and shall say all manner of evil against you falsely, for my sake. For great is your reward in Heaven.

He knows everything there is to know about you,
He'll walk right in front of you, to always protect you,
So the devil can't do you no harm,
because he's that kind of friend. —TRAMAINE HAWKINS

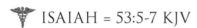 ISAIAH = 53:5-7 KJV

> He was wounded for our transgressions he was bruised for
> our iniquities: The chastisement of our peace was upon him;
> and with his stripes we are healed...
> He was oppressed, and he was afflicted, yet he opened not his
> mouth; he is brought as a lamb to the slaughter and as a sheep
> before her shearers is dumb, so he openeth not his mouth.

 JEREMIAH = 8:22 KJV

> Is there no balm in Gilead, is there no physician there?
> Why then is not the health of the daughter of my people
> recovered?

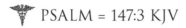 PSALM = 147:3 KJV

> He healeth the broken in heart and bindeth up their wounds.
> He telleth the number of the stars:
> He calleth them all by their names.
> Great is our Lord, and of great power: his understanding is
> infinite.

 PROVERB = 4:22 CEV

My words will give life, and Health to anyone who understands them.
Be careful how you think; your life is shaped by your thoughts.

 PROVERB = 3:8 KJV

It shall be health to thy navel, and marrow to thy bones.

Made by your hand, out the dust came man,
Form to your perfect plan, cause of you I can stand.
—PAUL PORTER

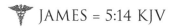 JAMES = 5:14 KJV

> Is any sick among you? Let him call for the Elders of the church; and let them pray over him, Anointing him with oil in the name of the Lord Jesus Christ.

HEBREWS = 4:12 CEV

> What God has said; is not only alive and active!
> It's sharper than any double two edged sword,
> His word can cut through our spirits and soul and through our joints and marrow, until it discover the desires and thoughts of our hearts. Nothing is hidden from God! He sees through everything, and we will have to give an account of what we've done and tell him the truth.

REVELATION=21:4 KJV

> God shall wipe away all tears from their eyes; and there shall be no more death, neither sorrow, nor crying, neither shall there be any more pain: For the former things are passed away.

PSALM =41:3KJV

> The Lord will strengthen him upon the bed of languishing; thou wilt make all his bed in his sickness.

 JEREMIAH = 17:14 KJV

Heal me, O Lord, and I shall be healed: save me, and I shall be saved: for thou art my praise.

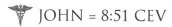 JOHN = 8:51 CEV

Jesus said, I tell you for certain that if you obey my words, you will never die

You are the potter, I am the clay. Mold and make me in thine own way. Once a seed, but now a flower, shower me with your holy power.
—PAUL PORTER

 PROVERBS = 17:22 KJV

A merry heart doeth good like a medicine: but a broken spirit drieth the bones.

 PSALM = 118:17 KJV

I shall not die, but live, and declare, the work of the Lord. The Lord hath chastened me sore: but he hath not given me over unto death.

 JAMES = 5:15 KJV

The prayer of faith shall save the sick; and the Lord shall raise him up, and if he have committed sins they shall be forgiven him.

 MATTHEW = 10:1 KJV

Jesus called together his twelve (12) disciples. He gave them the power to force out evil spirits, and to heal every kind of disease, and sickness.

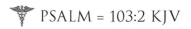 PSALM = 103:2 KJV

> Bless the Lord, O my soul, and forget not all his benefits. Who for giveth all thine iniquities; who healeth all our diseases.

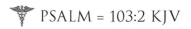 MALACHI = 4:2 KJV

> Unto you that fear my name shall the Sun of righteousness arise with healing in his wings.

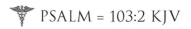 JEREMIAH = 30:17 KJV

> For I will restore health unto you, and I will heal thee of thy wounds, saith the LORD:

Weeping may endure for a night,
Keep the faith, it'll be alright,
cause trouble don't last always.
—REV. TIMOTHY WRIGHT

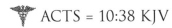 ACTS = 10:38 KJV

How God anointed Jesus Christ of Nazareth with the Holy Ghost, and with power. Who went about doing good, and healing all that were oppressed of the devil.

REVELATION = 12:11 KJV

They overcame the devil by the blood of the lamb and by the word of their testimony.

JEREMIAH = 33:6 KJV

Behold, I will bring it health and cure, and I will cure them, and will reveal unto them the abundance of peace and truth.

MARK = 9:23 KJV

If thou canst believe, all things are possible to him that believeth.

 MARK = 1:40 KJV

There came a leper to Jesus saying; If thou will, thou can make me clean. Jesus said; I will, be thou clean.

 COLOSSIANS = 2:2 KJV

That their hearts might be comforted being knit together in love, and unto all riches of the full assurance of understanding to the acknowledgement of the mystery of God, and of the Father, and of Jesus Christ. In whom are hid all the treasures of wisdom and knowledge.

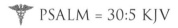 PSALM = 30:5 KJV

Weeping may endure for a night, but joy cometh in the morning.

Our Precious Redeemer, each toil will repay
It pays to serve Jesus, each and every day.
—FRANK C. HUSTON

 PSALM = 16:11 KJV

Thou wilt shew me the path of life: In thy presence is fullness of joy: at thy right hand there are pleasure forever more.

 PSALM = 16:10 KJV/CEV

I am your chosen one: Lord you won't leave me in the grave or let my body decay. For thou wilt not leave my soul in hell: neither wilt thou suffer thine Holy One to see corruption.

 ISAIAH = 25:8 KJV

He will swallow up death in victory: and the Lord God will wipe away tears from off all faces and the rebuke of his people shall he take away from off all the earth for the Lord had spoken it.

 JEREMIAH =31:3 KJV

I have loved you with an everlasting love, Therefore with loving Kindness have I drawn thee.

 HAGGAI =2:9 KJV

The glory of this latter house shall be greater than of the former, saith the Lord of hosts; and in this place will I give peace, saith the Lord of hosts.

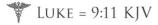 LUKE = 9:11 KJV

The people, when they knew it, followed him; and he received them, and spake unto them of the kingdom of God, and healed them that had need of Healing.

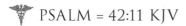 PSALM = 42:11 KJV

Why art thou cast down, O my soul? And why art thou disquieted within me? Hope thou in God: for I shall yet praise him, who is the health of my countenance, and my God.

This too shall pass
Scars will heal, you'll love again
God's purpose soon, you'll understand.
So when the pain, comes to an end.
Help someone to love again. —YOLANDER ADAMS

 EXODUS = 15:26 KJV

> If thou will diligently hearken to the voice of the Lord thy God; and will do that which is right in his sight and will give ear to his commandments and keep all his statutes, I will put none of these diseases upon you, which I have brought upon the Egyptians; for I am the Lord that healeth thee:

DEUTERONOMY = 7:15 KJV

> The Lord will take away from you all sickness, and will put none of the evil diseases of Egypt, which thou knowest, upon thee; but will lay them upon all them that hate thee...

HEBREWS = 10:14 GNT

> Because of Jesus sacrifice, we are now made perfect, forever. saved, sanctified and filled with the precious Holy Ghost..

PSALM = 27:1 KJV

> The Lord is my light and my salvation; whom shall I fear?
> The Lord is the strength of my life of whom shall I be afraid?

❦ JOB = 38:12 KJV

Has thou commanded the morning since thy days; and caused the dayspring to know his place.

❦ ACTS = 27:34 KJV

Wherefore I pray you to take some meat; for this is for your health:
For there shall not an hair fall from the head of any of you.

❦ PROVERB = 4:22 KJV

My words, for they are life unto those that find them, and health to all their flesh.

HEALING SPIRITUAL SCRIPTURES 100

It pays to serve Jesus, every step of the way
It pays to serve him each and every day.
—FRANK C. HUSTON

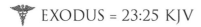 EXODUS = 23:25 KJV

Serve the Lord your God; and he shall bless thy bread, and thy water, and I will take sickness away from the midst of thee.

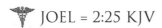 JOEL = 2:25 KJV

I will restore to you the years that the locust hath eaten, the cankerworm, and the caterpillar and the palmerworm, my great army which I sent among you. And you shall eat in plenty and be satisified and praise the name of the Lord your God, that dealt wondrously with you: and my people shall never be ashamed.

PROVERBS = 16: 24 KJV

Pleasant words are as an honeycomb, sweet to the soul, and health to the bones...

JOHN = 4:24 KJV

God is a Spirit; and they that worship him must worship him in Spirit and in truth.

 I CORINTHIANS = 3:21 KJV

Therefore let no man glory in men. For all things are yours, and ye are Christ's; and Christ is God's.

 PROVERBS = 12:18 KJV

The Tongue of the wise is health. Sharp words cut like a sword, but words of wisdom heal.

PROVERBS =13:3 KJV

He that keepeth his mouth keepeth his life; but he that openeth wide his lips shall have destruction.

HEALINGS SPIRITUAL SCRIPTURES 101

There's a balm in Gilead to make the wounded whole,
There's a balm in Gilead to heal the sin sick soul.
If you can't preach like Peter, If you can't pray like Paul, You can tell
the love of Jesus, and say, "He died for all." Traditional Spirituals

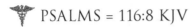 PSALMS = 116:8 KJV

> For thou hast delivered my soul from death, mine eyes from
> tears and my feet from falling. I will walk before the Lord in
> the land of the living.

ROMANS = 8:11 KJV

> If the spirit of him that raised up Jesus from the dead dwell in
> you, he that raised up Christ from the dead shall also quicken
> your mortal bodies by his spirit that dwelleth in you.

1 PETER = 2:24 KJV

> Who his own self bare our sins in his own body on the tree;
> that we being dead to sin should live unto righteousness, by
> whose stripes you were healed.

I THESSALONIANS = 4:16 KJV

> For the Lord himself shall descend from heaven with a shout,
> with the voice of the archangel, and with the trump of God:
> and the dead in Christ shall rise first.

I THESSALONIANS = 4:17 KJV

Then we which are alive and remain shall be caught up together with them in the clouds, to meet the Lord in the air: and so shall we forever be with the Lord. The Rapture!

You didn't see fit to let, none of these things be
Every day by your power, you keep on keeping me.
Thank you Lord, for all you've done for me.
—WALTER HAWKINS

 JAMES = 5:16 KJV

> Confess your faults one to another and pray one for another that you may be healed, The effectual fervent prayer of a righteous man availeth much.

 PROVERBS = 15:13 KJV

> A merry heart maketh a cheerful countenance, but by sorrow of the heart the spirit is broken.

 JEREMIAH = 30:17 KJV

> I will restore health unto you and I will heal thee of thy wounds, saith the Lord.

 PROVERBS = 3:2 KJV

> For length of days and long life, and peace shall they add to thee. Let not mercy and truth forsake thee...

 PROVERBS = 18:10 KJV

The Lord is like a strong tower where the righteous can go
and be safe.

 PROVERBS = 18:14 KJV

Your will to live, can sustain you, when you are sick, but if you
lose it, your last hope is gone.

PROVERBS = 4:23 KJV

Keep thy heart with all dilligence; for out of it are the issues
of life.

One day when I was lost, He died upon the cross.
They pierced him in his side; He hung his head and died
I know it was the blood for me. Traditional Spirituals

☤ ISAIAH = 41:10 KJV

> Fear thou not; for I am with thee: be not dismayed; for I am
> thy God: I will strengthen thee; Yea, I will help thee; Yes I will
> uphold thee with the right hand of my righteousness.

☤ MATTHEW = 8:16 KJV

> When the evening came, They brought unto him many that
> were possessed with devils: and he cast out spirits with only a
> word he forced out evil spirits and healed everyone who was
> sick that it might be fulfilled which was spoken by Isaiah the
> prophet, saying "(Himself took our infirmities, and bare our
> sickness."

☤ NAHUM = 1:9 KJV

> What do you imagine against the Lord? He will make an utter
> end: affliction shall not rise up the second time.

☤ EPHESIANS = 1:13 KJV

> In whom you also trusted, after that you heard the word of
> truth, the gospel of your salvation; in whom also after that
> you believed, you were sealed with that holy Spirit of promise.

 COLOSSIANS= 1:28 KJV

That we may present every man perfect in Christ Jesus.

 HEBREWS = 12:23 KJV

To the general assembly and church of the firstborn, which are written in heaven, and to God the Judge of all, and to the spirits of just men made perfect.

I could have been dead, sleeping in my grave.
But you healed my body, and made my enemies behave.
Traditional Spirituals

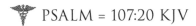 PSALM = 107:20 KJV

>He sent his word, and healed them, and delivered them from their destructions.

ROMANS = 8:26 KJV

>In certain ways we are weak, but the spirit is here to help us.
>For example when we don't know what to pray for,
>The spirit prays for us in ways that cannot be put into words.
>All of our thoughts are known to God, He can understand what is in the mind of the spirit, as the spirit prays for God's people.

2 CORINTHIANS = 4:17 KJV

>For our light affliction, which is, but for a moment,
>worketh for us a far more exceeding and eternal weight of glory.

ROMANS = 4:8 KJV

>Blessed is the man to whom the Lord will not impute sin.

MATTHEW = 4:23 KJV - MATTHEW = 9:35 KJV

Jesus went about all the cities and villages, teaching in their synagogues, and preaching the gospel of the kingdom, and healing every sickness and every disease. The people were astonished at his doctrine.

 EZEKIEL = 37:3 KJV

The Lord God said unto me, can these bones live?
Prophesy upon these bones, and behold they shall live!

Come ye broken hearted, come ye weary soul.
There's healing water that can make you whole.
—Traditional Spirituals

 2 KINGS=5:14 KJV

Na-aman captain of the king of Syria, wanted to recover from leprosy. He came unto Israel, and Elisha; said: Go and wash in the Jordan river (7) seven times, and thy will be clean. Then he went down, and dipped himself seven times in the Jordan river, and his flesh came again like unto the flesh of a little child and he was healed of leprosy.

ISAIAH = 38:1 KJV

The prophet Isaiah, said unto King Hezekiah, get your house in order; for thou shall die and not live. Then Hezekiah turned his face toward the wall, and prayed. Then the Lord God said; I have heard your prayers, I have seen your tears, behold I will add unto thy days fifteens (15) years, and I will deliver thee and this city out of the hand of thy enemy.

LUKE = 17:6 CEV

Jesus said, If you had faith as a grain of mustard seed, you can Prophesy unto this sycamine tree, be thou plucked up by the root, and be thou planted in the sea; and it should obey you.

There is a name I love to hear, I love to sing it's worth;
It sound like music in my ear, the sweetest name on earth,
O' how I love Jesus! O' how I love Jesus!
—FREDERICK WHITFIELD

✾ ISAIAH = 61:1 KJV

> The Spirit of the Lord God is upon me: because the Lord
> hath anointed me to preach the gospel to the poor; He hath
> sent me to bind up the brokenhearted, to proclaim liberty to
> the captives, and the opening of the prison to them that are
> bound; To proclaim the acceptable year of the Lord, and the
> day of vengeance of our God; to comfort all that mourn: To
> appoint unto them that mourn in Zion, to give unto them
> beauty for ashes, the oil of joy for mourning, the garment of
> praise for the spirit of heaviness; that they might be called
> trees of righteousness, the planting of the Lord, that he might
> be Glorified.

✾ PSALM = 23:1 KJV

> The lord is my shepherd; I shall not want. He maketh me
> to lie down in green pastures: he leadeth me beside the still
> waters. He restoreth my soul: He leadeth me in the paths of
> righteousness for his name's sake. Yea, though I walk through
> the valley of the shadow of death, I will fear no evil: for thou
> art with me: thy rod and thy staff they comfort me. Thou
> preparest a table before me in the presence of mine enemies:
> Thou anointest my head with oil; my cup runneth over. Surely
> goodness and mercy shall follow me all the days of my life.
> And I will dwell in the house of the Lord forever.

I CORINTHIANS = 15:53 KJV

For this corruptible must put on incorruption, and this mortal must put on immortality. So when this corruptible shall have put on incorruption, and this mortal shall have put on immortality, then shall be brought to pass the saying that is written; Death is swallowed up in victory. O' death where is thy victory! For we are VICTORIOUS in CHRIST!

I Love you, Jesus - I worship and adore you.
Just want to tell you, that I love you, more than anything!
—Traditional Spirituals

♫ PSALM = 91:1 KJV

He that dwelleth in the secret place of the most High shall abide under the shadow of the Almighty. I will say of the Lord, He is my refuge and my fortress: my God; in him will I trust. Surely he shall deliver thee from the snare of the fowler, and from the noisome pestilence. He shall cover thee with his feathers, and under his wings shall thou trust: his truth shall be thy shield and buckler. Thou shalt not be afraid for the terror by night; nor for the arrow that flieth by day; Nor for the destruction that wasteth at noonday, A thousand shall fall at thy side, and ten thousand at thy right hand; but it shall not come nigh thee. Only with thine eyes shalt thou behold and see the reward of the wicked. Because thou hast made the Lord, which is my refuge, even the most High thy habitation; There shall no evil befall thee. Neither shall any plague come nigh thy dwelling. For he shall give his angels charge over thee, to keep thee in all thy ways. They shall bear thee up in their hands lest thou dash thy foot against a stone. Thou shalt tread upon the lion and adder; the young lion and the dragon shalt thou trample under feet. Because he hath set his love upon me. Therefore will I deliver him; I will set him on high, because he hath known my name, He shall call upon me, and I will answer him; I will be with him in trouble I will deliver him, and honour him with long life will I satisfy him and show him my salvation.

🙏 JOB = 22:28 KJV

Declaration of Authoritative orders Thou shalt also Decree a thing, and it shall be established unto you; and the light shall shine upon thy ways.

🙏 PSALM = 2:7 KJV

I will Declare the Decree: the Lord hath said unto me, Thou art my Son; this day have I begotten thee.
Decree, Declare, Demand, Command, Condemn and Compel. These are spiritual attributes to obtain for spiritual warfare.

Decree- a formal and authoritative order, especially one having the force of law.

Declare- to make a declaration; to state officially or formally or affirm authority.

Command- is an order that you have to follow as long as the person has authority over you.

Compel- to obtain or bring about by force; to submit, subdue or cast out.
Condemn- to pronounce judgement against; to sentence to doom = hell.

The person making the decree must be in a position of power and authority to do so. You have the power and authority to make decrees, and expect that, they will be carried out. You shall decree, the power is yours, state your case and write out the conditions regarding your home, family, ministry and all that concerns you. The words that you speak will be established; that means it will be manifested reveal, and showed to be true. As you have spoken it. The light shall shine upon thy way which means there will be enlightment in your mind, and spirit that will cause you to see clearly the path that is laid before you. You will nor stumble about in darkness, walk timidly, and unsure, but will have clarity, purpose and direction.

Therefore you have the power, and the authority to speak out a thing in your life and expect to see it manifested in the reality of your world. What you decree you should also declare- that is to speak empathetically and to make known, and clearly state your position upon the matter. In order to both decree and declare a thing and expect to see the manifestation you must know the word of God, so you'll understand your legal right to have your decree upheld.
There are always condition that you must meet in order to have the authority to do anything in the kingdom of God.

♫ DEUTERONOMY=28:1

states; It shall come to pass if thou shalt hearkend diligently unto the voice of the Lord thy God to observe and to do all his commandments which I command thee this day. That the Lord thy God will set thee on high above all nations of the earth; When you hear, receive, and obey the word of God you are given the power to decree the word. Speak the answer; not the problem. The answer is in the word of God... Read your bible, and ask the Holy Ghost for assistance, and guidance as to what you need to decree in your life on behalf of your families, ministries, city, government, and nation. There is a word in the word of God that holds the answer to your question. You must understand the principle behind decreeing and declaring the word of God. You must meet the condition;

read, hear, obey, and speak the word. Believe and expect to see the manifestation. Know that you have the right to legislate, and cause change to come based on the power, and dominion that God has given you. Jesus finished it on the cross, now all your work is done on your knees in prayer, and the Holy Ghost will reveal to you what to decree and declare. Stop telling God about your problems, and tell your problem about your God! God has to have your consent to bless you, and Satan has to have your consent to curse you; so be careful about what you say and do. What you watch, and what you listen to, can give Satan access to your authority. No one can praise God for you, Luke= 19:40 if they hold their peace, the very rocks shall cry out. You must praise him for yourself. Praise give God the right or the consent to bless you, so open your mouth, and begin to bless him! Yes you can praise him at home or all alone, but are you ashamed to bless God in front of other believers. God loved king David because he was not ashamed to bless God in front of others such as Goliath! You don't have to be a giant, - to be a giant slayer!

We have Power and Spiritual Authority, We are supernaturally and Spirituality beings. The reason demons tempts us to sin is so we become powerless in their present. Just as Superman is powerless to Krytonite, so are we powerless to Satan, when we sin. Don't let him walk beside you were he can whisper in your ear nor behind you, but he belongs under your feet. Jesus knew no sin. Jesus exercised his authority by forcing the demons out.

MATTHEW = 8:31

So the devils besought Jesus, saying if thou cast us out; suffer us to go away into the herd of swine; and, Jesus cast them out!

I DECREE AND DECLARE IT, BY THE POWER OF THE HOLY GHOST IN THE NAME OF JESUS!

LUKE = 21: 19

In your patience possess ye your souls.

❧ ISAIAH = 14:12 KJV

SATAN

How art thou fallen from heaven, O Lu'-ci-fer, son of the morning! How art thou cut down to the ground, which didst weaken the nations! For thou hast said in thine heart, I will ascend into heaven,
I will exalt my throne above the stars of God:
I will sit also upon the mount of the congregation, in the side of the north:
I will ascend above the heights of the clouds:
I will be like the most High God. Yet thou shalt be brought down to hell, to the sides of the pit. They that see thee shall narrowly look upon thee, and consider thee, saying, Is this the man that made the earth to tremble, that did shake kingdoms; That made the world as a wilderness, and destroyed the cities there of; that opened not the house of his prisoners?

All the kings of the nations, even all of them, lie in glory, everyone in his own house. But thou art cast out of thy grave like an abominable branch, and as the raiment of those that are slain, thrust through with a sword, that go down to the stones of the pit; as a carcase trodden under feet. Thou shalt not be joined with them in burial, because thou hast destroyed thy land, and slain thy people: the seed of evildoers shall never be renowned.

☙ EZEKIEL =28:2-19 KJV

SATAN; THE KING OF TYRUS!

Prophecy against, Satan; the king of Tyrus.

Thus saith the Lord God; because thine heart is lifted up with pride, you claim to be a god.

You say that like a god, you sit on a throne surrounded by the seas; you may pretend to be a god, but no you are mortal, not divine; You think you are wiser than Daniel, that no secret can be kept from you. Your wisdom and skill made you rich with treasure of gold and silver. You made clever business deals and kept on making profits, how proud you are of your wealth! Now then, this is what I the Lord God, am saying; because you think you are as wise as a god. I will bring ruthless enemies to attack you. They will destroy all the beautiful things you have acquired by skill, and wisdom. They will kill you, and send you to a watery grave. When they come to kill you, will you still claim that you are a god? When you face your murderers, you will be mortal and not at all divine. You will be like a dog at the hand of godless strangers, I the Lord God have given the command.

You were once full of wisdom and perfect in beauty, an example of perfection. You lived in the Garden of Eden, and wore gems of every kind; diamonds, emeralds, rubbies, sapphires, jasper, and gold; The workmanship of thy tabrets and of thy pipes was prepared in thee in the day that thou was created. Thou art the Anointed Cherub that covereth.

You lived on my holy mountain, and walked among sparkling gems. Your conduct was perfect from the day you were created until you began to do evil.

You were busy buying, and selling, and this led you to violence, and sin so I forced you to leave my holy mountain, and the angel who guarded you, drove you away from the sparking gems. You were proud of being handsome, and your fame made you act like a fool, because of this I hurled you to the ground, and left you as a warning to other kings.

You did such evil in buying, and selling that your places of worship were corrupted, so I set fire to the city, and burned it to the ground. All who look at you now see you reduced to ashes. You are gone, gone forever, and all the nations that had come to know you are terrified, afraid that they will share your fate. Satan, fall came about because of pride. He was the covering Cherubs; Cherubims and Seraphims are Angels in Heaven.

❧ REVELATION=12:7 KJV

SATAN'S END:

There was war in Heaven. "Mi-cha-el and his Angels fought against the dragon; and the dragon fought, and his angels, and prevailed not; neither was their place found any more in Heaven. And the great dragon was cast out, that old serpent, called the devil, and Satan, which deceiveth the whole world; he was cast out into the earth, and his angels were cast out with him. And I heard a loud voice saying in heaven, Now is come salvation, and strength, and the kingdom of our God, and the power of his Christ: for the accuser of our brethren is cast down, which accused them before our God day and night. And they overcome him by the blood of the Lamb, and by the word of their testimony; and they loved not their lives unto the death. Therefore rejoice, ye heavens, and ye that dwell in them. Woe to the inhabiters of the earth and of the sea! For the devil is come down unto you, having great wrath, because he knoweth that he hath, but a short time.

EXODUS=20:1 KJV

THE TEN COMMANDMENTS:

1. Thou shalt have no other gods before me.
2. Thou shalt not make unto thee any graven image.
3. Thou shalt not take the name of the Lord thy God in vain.
4. Remember the sabbath day and keep it holy.
5. Honour thy father and thy mother: that thy days may be long
6. Thou shalt not kill.
7. Thou shalt not commit adultery.
8. Thou shalt not steal.
9. Thou shalt not bear false witness against thy neighbour.
10. Thou shalt not covet thy neighbors assets.

THE AUTHOR'S PRAYER 113

"Most Holy; gracious eternal Father: We come before your holy presence, with praise of Thanksgiving; Thanking you for all your bountiful blessing, Thanking you for your peace, your joy, your salvation, your grace, your mercy, and your never ending love.

Thank you for all your blessing from above, for you've been better to us than we've been to ourselves. Ten (10) Thousand, on Ten (10) Thousand tongues can't thank you enough, you woke us up this morning, you started us on our way, put clothes on our backs, shoes on our feet, food on our tables, truly Lord, you are able. Able to open blinded eyes, able to open doors closed in our face, able to make a way out of no way. Lord, you're a way maker. We thank you for your son Jesus, who suffered, bled, and died on calvary cross, but on the (3rd) third day, He rose with all power in his hand, and now He's seated on the right hand side of the father, interceding on our behalves ascended into heaven, descended the power of the Holy Ghost.

Holy Spirit, rest, rule, and abide in us, lead us, and guide us in all truth, understanding, and knowledge of the father that we may be pleasing in thy sight, "O my strength, and my redeemer.

We pray that your Angels of protection be camp around this nation, my pastor, my church, my family, my home, my life, and my wife. Shield us from seen, and unseen dangers, and on the highways and the byways of this life.

Let no hurt, harm, danger, nor any accidents come unto us.
Bless us to be a blessing, hide us behind calvary cross,
that the people see less of us, and more of thee.
We thank you for the wisdom of your word in Jesus name.
Amen.....

THE AUTHOR'S POEM 114

"KEEP THY SIGHT ON NOTHING LESS"

I climbed the tallest tree, as I reach the top, two angels met me. They said; set thy sight on things above, and be filled with the saviors love.

Let go, and let God set you free, that's when we flew over the sea. Amazing grace, and Mercy to be found.

That's when I knew I was back on solid ground.

The new friends of the light, disappeared from sight, with thoughts of knowing how to deal with the night.

Now I know the power of love, let's you, and I think on things from above.

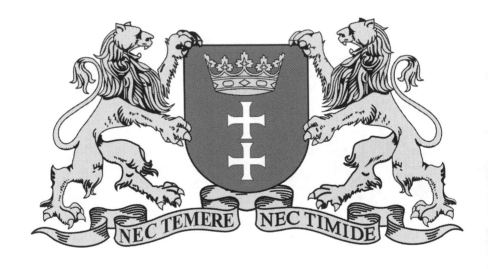

Printed in the United States
By Bookmasters